IN THE BEGINNING, THERE WERE STORIES

*Thoughts about
the Oral Tradition
of the Bible*

WILLIAM J. BAUSCH

IN THE
BEGINNING,
THERE WERE
STORIES

*Thoughts about
the Oral Tradition
of the Bible*

TWENTY-THIRD PUBLICATIONS

185 WILLOW STREET • PO BOX 180 • MYSTIC, CT 06355
TEL: 1-800-321-0411 • FAX: 1-800-572-0788
E-MAIL: ttpubs@aol.com • www.twentythirdpublications.com

DEDICATION

For Joan and Joe Henderson,
exceedingly generous in time, treasure and talent.

Twenty-Third Publications
A Division of Bayard
185 Willow Street
P.O. Box 180
Mystic, CT 06355
(860) 536-2611 or (800) 321-0411
www.twentythirdpublications.com
ISBN:1-58595-361-X

Library of Congress Catalog Card Number: 2004107023
Printed in the U.S.A.

CONTENTS

INTRODUCTION

The Bible is a messy collection. In its original form it had no chapters, no verses, and no punctuation; all the words ran together. It was a real art to know where to separate everything, where put a period and begin another sentence.

The Bible consists of seventy-two books of varied style, running the gamut from history to fiction to poetry. We don't know who the majority of authors were—and this includes the gospel writers. It's probably safe to say that each book was written by a "committee" over a long period of time. Each is a composite venture with many authors who enlarged, amended, edited, changed, deleted, interpreted, and corrected the texts.

The biblical books were written in three different languages and in an entirely different culture whose values and understandings are almost completely opposite to ours. And this is what we want to explore! It's like entering Wonderland with Alice: nothing is quite what it seems.

The point of this book, then, is to remind the reader that before the books of the Bible were written down, they were spoken. In other words, behind the print there is a long, long oral tradition that comes through in the written text. This oral tradition is the key to understanding the Bible and, as we shall see, we must really unlearn our modern literary prejudices and adapt the ancient oral mentality if we are to deal with the variety of styles, the errors in content, the contradictions, and the colorful dynamics of the Bible.

This book is presented in three parts. In Part I we clear the air and deal with some preliminaries we absolutely need to look at before we proceed. Here we will examine four themes: revelation, truth wrapped in story, the slow and disastrous tyranny of written print over oral story, and the chasm between the biblical culture and ours. In Part II, we'll move on to our primary concern of unlocking the mysteries of the Bible by using a special key, which is called story. In Part III, we take a brief look at biblical history, both sacred and profane.

I must firmly stress that this storytelling key is only one approach to understanding the Bible. As such, it has its limitations. The reader should look elsewhere for a fuller and deeper understanding of Scripture. Furthermore, I must confess that scriptural exegesis is not my forte; in fact, I am fairly ignorant of it. But I am a parish priest and a storyteller and, after all, when you come right down to it, the Bible is a collection of stories. And when you apply storytelling principles to interpreting Scripture, you'll be surprised what you can learn. As the old saying goes, tell me the stories that fill your life and I'll tell you who you are. The Bible stories tell us who the ancient Hebrews and early Christians are—and by extension, who we are or should be.

I wish to acknowledge my indebtedness to the following whose books and thoughts I have principally raided: the works of Raymond Brown, SS, Bruce J. Malina, John J. Pilch, and James L. Kugel. I am especially indebted to the works of James D. G. Dunn, Kevin M. Bradt, Sidney Lumet, and Barbara E. Organ. Finally, I have relied on my own past books on storytelling—which themselves pay homage to many storytellers throughout the ages.

Part I

THE SCRIBAL PREJUDICE

1.

REVELATION

John and Martha were practicing Catholics who were looking around for a parish to join. They found a parish nearby to their home, but had yet to meet the pastor who was away. Meanwhile, they found out that their elderly neighbor, Mary, who lived all alone, was a churchgoer. So one day, John and Martha invited Mary over to dinner. As they sat in the living room, in the afterglow of a delicious meal, the couple asked Mary about the pastor at the nearby parish. What kind of man was he? Mary was silent for a long time and then finally said, "You want to know the kind of man your pastor is? It's hard to put into words." She paused and said, "If you don't mind, let me share a story about him and you draw your own conclusions." Martha and John settled in, as Mary went on:

There was a terrible storm that year. I remember it well. For three days a fierce winter storm had traveled 1,500 miles across the North Pacific from Alaska, packing gale force winds and torrential rains. In the Sierra Nevada Mountains to the east, the snow was piling up. The streets were flooded, and in some parts of town, the power was off where trees had blown down. At our small church, the heavy rain and high winds beat against the windows with a violence that Father O'Malley said he had never before heard. He was in his tiny bedroom writing his Sunday's sermon by candlelight.

Out of the darkness the phone in his office rang, shattering his concentration. He picked up the candle, and with his hand cupped in front of it, ambled down the hall. As he picked up the phone, a voice quickly asked, "Is this Father O'Malley?" "Yes." "I'm calling from the hospital in Auburn," said a concerned female voice. "We have a terminally ill patient who is asking us to get someone to give him his last rites. Can you come quickly?" "I'll try my best to make it," Father O'Malley answered. "But the river is over its banks, and trees are blown down all over town. It's the worst storm I've seen in all the years I've been here. Look for me within two hours."

The trip was only thirty miles, but it would be hard going. The headlights on Father O'Malley's twenty-year-old car barely penetrated the slashing rain, and where the winding road crossed and recrossed the river in a series of small bridges, trees had blown down across the river's banks. But for some reason, there was always just enough room for Father O'Malley to maneuver his way around them. His progress was slow and cautious, but he continued on toward the hospital. Finally, in the near distance, the lights of the small hospital served as a beacon to guide O'Malley for the last 500 yards, and he hoped he had arrived in time. He parked behind the three other cars in the parking lot to avoid as much wind as possible. With his tattered ritual book tucked deep inside his overcoat pocket, O'Malley forced the car door open, stepped out, and then leaned into the wind. Its power almost bowled him over, and he was nearly blown away from the hospital entrance.

Once inside, the wind slammed the hospital door shut

behind him, and as he was shaking the water from his coat, he heard footsteps headed his way. It was the night nurse. "I'm so glad you could get here," she said. "The man I called about is slipping fast, but he is still coherent. He's been an alcoholic for years, and his liver has finally given out. He's been here for a couple of weeks this time and hasn't had one single visitor. He lives up in the woods, and no one around here knows much about him. He always pays his bill with cash and doesn't seem to want to talk much. We've been treating him off and on for the last couple of years, but this time it's as though he's reached some personal decision and has given up the fight." "What's your patient's name?" Father O'Malley asked. "The hospital staff has just been calling him Tom," she replied.

In the soft night-light of the room, Tom's thin sallow countenance looked ghostlike behind a scraggly beard. It was as though he had stepped over the threshold and his life was already gone. "Hello, Tom. I'm Father O'Malley. I was passing by and thought we could talk a bit before you go to sleep for the night." "Don't give me any of that garbage," Tom replied. "You didn't just stop by at 3:30 in the morning. I asked that dumb night nurse to call someone to give me my last rites because I know my deal is done and it's my turn to go. Now get on with it." "Patience," said Father O'Malley, and he began to say the prayers of the last rites. After the "Amen," Tom perked up a bit, and he seemed to want to talk.

"Would you like to make your confession?" O'Malley asked him. "Absolutely not," Tom answered. "But I would like to just talk with you a bit, before I go." And so Tom and Father O'Malley talked about the Korean War, and the ferocity of the winter storm, and the knee-high grass and summer blossoms that would soon follow. Occasionally, during the hour or so before daylight, Father O'Malley would ask Tom again, "Are you sure you don't want to confess anything?" After a couple of hours, and after about the fourth or fifth time that Father O'Malley asked the same question, Tom replied, "Father, when I was young, I did something that was so bad that I've never told anyone about it. It was so bad that I haven't spent a single day since without thinking about it and reliving the horror." "Don't you think it would be good for you to tell me about it?" O'Malley asked. "Even now, I still can't talk about what I did," Tom said. "Even to you."

But as the first gray light of dawn crept into the room and began to form shadows, Tom sadly said, "Okay. It's too late for anyone to do anything to me now, so I guess I might as well tell you. I worked as a switchman on the railroad all my life, until I retired a few years ago and moved up here to the woods. Thirty-two years, two months, and eleven days ago, I was working in Bakersfield on a night kind of like tonight." Tom's face became intense as the words began to tumble out. "It happened during a bad winter storm with a lot of rain, fifty-mile-an-hour winds and almost no visibility. It was two nights before Christmas and to push away the gloom, the whole yard crew drank all through the swing shift. I was drunker than the rest of them, so I volunteered to go out in the rain and wind and push the switch for the northbound 8:30 freight."

Tom's voice dropped almost to a whisper as he went on. "I guess I was more drunk than I thought I was because I pushed that switch in the wrong direction. At forty-five miles an hour that freight train slammed into a passenger car at the next crossing and killed a young man, his wife, and their two daughters. I have had to live with my being the cause of their deaths every day since then." There was a long moment of silence as Tom's confession of this tragedy hung in the air. After what seemed like an eternity, Father O'Malley gently put his hand on Tom's shoulder and said very quietly, "If I can forgive you, God can forgive you because in that car were my mother, my father and my two older sisters."

—Modified from *Chicken Soup for the Christian Soul*

John and Mary sat speechless. Finally, John said, "Quite a story. Quite a man. How do you know all this?" Mary smiled and said simply, "I was there. I was the nurse who called him." And John and Mary smiled for they had learned what kind of a man their new pastor was.

Dismantling the Story

Quite a lovely and moving story Mary told. There are a lot of lessons in it. With justification an exegete (one who parses, or takes apart, stories for meaning) could develop several dissertations on courage or forgiveness, virtues that are quite apparent in the story. He or she could even arrive at valuable definitions of these virtues, break them down, and systematize them. Or one could tackle the issue of sin, discussing Tom's sins and putting them into categories of seriousness—are they mortal or venial (does anyone even remember those distinctions anymore)? Our exegete could probably draw numerous conclusions from this story. But, as helpful as that might be, it would miss the point.

The point of the story is this: what kind of man is the pastor? Mary could have replied to John and Martha's inquiry with generalizations—Father O'Malley is dedicated, kind, and forgiving. Instead, Mary choose a time-honored way of replying: she told a story and in the story there was not doctrine or proposition, not creed or code, but revelation, the revelation of a person through storytelling.

The Bible is fundamentally a book of revelation. That's a new concept for many because when the average person thinks of revelation, he or she likely thinks of a tangible proposition handed down from on high, a divine statement of something we never knew before. For most people biblical revelation is like catching the map to Captain Kidd's treasure as it floats down from heaven, or learning the secret revealed to the children at Fatima, or hearing the Wizard proclaim, " I am Oz!" That's revelation! As the average person sees it, eventually over all these the centuries, these divine exposures have been collected into an anthology called the Bible. In turn, these revelations are parceled out in digestible packages, known as dogmas and doctrines, by those in charge of revealing the revelations—that is, the Church. One "comes to faith" by learning, memorizing, and accepting the doctrines, and by being able to repeat them back.

To put it another way, God spoke to the biblical authors, who in turn wrote down God's words. The Church, the guardian of those recorded and eventually reinterpreted words, then reset them in neat, classified systematic propositions called doctrines as the fixed, inviolable "deposit of faith" or collection of objective truths. This was revelation and tradition at work under an official Church office whose special responsibility was keeping all the doctrines straight (orthodox). The result of all this was that in time revelation became *information* about God, not an *encounter* with God.

This "propositional" view of revelation held sway for many centuries, but it was always suspect. It made religion a matter of the head, of knowledge, of obedience to the Church and it often led to biblical and ecclesiastical fundamentalism. Then came the Second Vatican Council in the 1960s, which turned around this thinking and returned to the sources. Revelation was now deemed to be nothing more or less then what it was always meant to be: God's own self communication. From day one, as we shall note later, God has been revealed to all of humankind in nature, beauty, and the stirrings of the human heart. Consider the beautiful words of this poem by Charles Mary Plunkett:

> I see his blood upon the rose,
> And in the stars the glory of his eyes,
> His body gleams amid the eternal snows,
> His tears fall from the skies.
>
> I see his face in every flower;
> The thunder and the singing of the birds
> Are but his voice—and carven by his power
> Rocks are his written words.

All pathways by his feet are worn,
His strong heart stirs the ever-beating sea,
His crown of thorns is twined with every thorn.
His cross is every tree.

This may not be great poetry but it brings us much closer to the concept of revelation than do fixed propositions. In ancient times, revelation was understood as a generous exposure of God, a communicating invitation: "Here I am. This is who I am. Look at me. Come to me. Share my love." Revelation, in short, was about a person, not a statement; a lover, not a doctrine; a Father O'Malley (to return to our story above), not a treatise. It was not a transmission but an offer; not a proposition but a valentine. And, I repeat, revelation is, was, and always will be open to all.

Favorite Child

Just as a parent loves all her children, but sometimes has a special child with whom she especially resonates, so, too, God was revealed in a unique way to God's own special child, Israel (Ogden's Nash's verse "How odd/ of God/to choose/ the Jews" comes to mind here) without ceasing to love and call all other people. That self-exposure to Israel and its response, which ranged from joyous acceptance to wanton indifference, was orally passed on from generation to generation, then finally written down in what came to be known as the Bible. But even that was not enough for, "in the fullness of time," God was revealed once more in the person of Jesus. This was a definitive invitation, so much so that Jesus was called the "Word of God," and "the Word became flesh and lived among us, and we have seen his glory, the glory as of a father's only son, full of grace and truth" (Jn 1:14).

Remember that both in Israel and in Jesus, God's revelation was not a set of teachings or doctrines; it was always ""Here I am. This is who I am. Look at me. Come to me. Share my love.." In Jesus's death, revelation says, "Look, this is how far my love will go." And so in time the record of Israel, this "favorite child," became a privileged witness to God's love, and the definitive Jesus became the italicized word of all those recorded words God has been speaking to all people since time began: "How often have I desired to gather your children together as a hen gathers her brood under her wings" (Mt 23:37). Here once more was revelation, not as dogma but as person; not as information but as sharing.

At the risk of offending the reader, I have to say that that is what is wrong with the Christmas crèche, that sweet, adorable, and sentimental tableau of Jesus' birth. It deflects our attention away from the act of Incarnation, and focuses our imaginations on flourishes such as animals and angels, magi and shepherds, and a cooing, passive infant. To that extent the crèche is misleading. A homily I gave one Christmas tells you why:

A husband and wife, in their late eighties, both were becoming extremely forgetful. He would forget where he put his eyeglasses. Then as he went from room to room searching for them, he would forget what he was looking for. She would announce that she was going to the store for butter, but when she got there she would forget what she was shopping for. One evening, as they watched TV, the husband stood up. She says: where are you going? He says: To get snacks, it's my turn. She says: I want a hot fudge sundae. Write it down! He says: I don't have to write it down. She: And put nuts on it. Write it down! He: I don't have to write it down! She: And whipped cream on top. Write it down! He: I don't have to write it down.

The husband then left to get the snacks. When he returned, he presented his wife with a plate of bacon and eggs. She says: where's the toast?

People are forgetful. They even forget what this feast, Christmas, is about. Even good Christians forget. A recent poll conducted by the Lutherans, for example, found that the largest percentage of Christians interviewed said that Christmas was all about families getting together. Well, that's nice, but what about Christmas being about Jesus?

Even those who did mention Christmas as the birth of Christ, the founder of Christianity, tended to focus on the sentimentality of it all: the appealing baby in the manger, the adoring parents, the animals, shepherds, the choir of angels—the tableau of soft sweetness. Not one in a million, not even, I suspect, most of us here, would zone in on the one word—a rather shocking word—that the Bible, the Church, and tradition tell us is at the heart of Christmas.

That word is not sweetness, softness, gentleness. No, the word is *passion*! Does that surprise you? Yet it's written all over the Christmas scene. The truth of the matter is that we don't have in Christmas sweetness, softness, and gentleness. What we have here on this Christmas night is plain, unadulterated, hard, raw passion. What I'm challenging you to recall is that, yes, we have a cuddly baby, but behind that facade, behind that tenderness, is a fierce and a passionate God; that fact doesn't always come across in the sentimental pageantry of the manger.

Take a second look. The Christmas message and the Christmas celebration center around God's great love for us, the commitment not to leave us abandoned, not to leave us in the darkness of political, social, or personal tyrannies. The message of Christmas is summed up in the words the angel spoke to Mary at the annunciation: "You will name him Jesus," and he shall be known as Emmanuel, which translates "God with us." Yes, "God with us," or, in the reverential phrase of John's gospel, "*Et verbum caro factum est et habitavit in nobis*"—"And the Word was made flesh and dwelt among us."

Why? Why? Why does God want to dwell among us? Because God wants to. Because, simply put, the object of all love is union: to be with the beloved. So,whatever it is, God has a thing for us—a passion. The real Christmas memory, then, is not that of a passive, seductive baby Jesus but rather of an active, desiring God. Christmas is about a driving desire on God's part to dwell among us, to be a part of the human condition. God loves us that much. God yearns for us that much. And that's passion. Maybe I can get my point across through a story, a story that mentions a baby. It's told by a woman, the baby's mother. Listen.

It was Sunday, Christmas. Our family had spent a holiday in San Francisco with my husband's parents, but in order for us to be back at work on Monday, we found ourselves driving the 400 miles back home to Los Angeles on Christmas Day. We stopped for lunch in King City. The restaurant was nearly empty. We were the only family and ours were the only children. I heard Erik, my one-year-old, squeal with glee. "Hithere," the two words he always thought were one. "Hithere," and he pounded his fat baby hands whack, whack, whack on the metal high chair. His face was alive with excitement, his eyes were wide, gums bared in a toothless grin. He wriggled and giggled and then I saw the source of his merriment. A tattered rag of a coat, obviously bought by someone else eons ago, dirty, greasy, and worn; baggy pants; spindly body; toes that poked out of would-be shoes; a shirt that had ring-around-the-collar all over; and a face like none other gums as bare as Erik's. "Hi there, baby. Hi there, big boy, I see ya, Buster." My husband and I exchanged a look that was a cross between "What do we do?" and "Poor devil."

Our meal came and the banging and the noise continued. Now the old bum was shouting across the room, "Do you know patty cake? Atta boy. Do you know peek-a-boo? Hey, look! He knows peek-a-boo!" Erik continued to laugh and answer, "Hithere." Every call was echoed. Nobody thought it was cute. The guy was a drunk and a disturbance. I was embarrassed. My husband, Dennis, was humiliated. Even our six-year-old said, "Why is that old man talking so loud?"

Dennis went to pay the check, imploring me to get Erik and meet him in the parking lot. "Lord, just let me get out of here before he speaks to me or Erik," and I bolted for the door. It soon was obvious that both the Lord and Erik had other plans. As I drew closer to the man, I turned my back, walking to side-step him and any air that he might be breathing. As I did so, Erik, all the while with his eyes riveted to his best friend, leaned over my arm, reaching with both arms to a baby's pick-me-up position. In a split second of balancing my baby and turning to counter his weight, I came eye-to-eye with the old man.

Erik was lunging for him, arms spread wide. The bum's eyes both asked and implored, "Would you let me hold your baby?" There was no need for me to answer since Erik propelled himself from my arms to the man. Suddenly a very old man and a very young baby consummated their love relationship. Erik laid his tiny head upon the man's ragged shoulder. The man's eyes closed and I saw tears hover beneath the lashes. His aged hands, full of grime and pain and hard labor, gently, so gently, cradled my baby's bottom and stroked his back. I stood awestruck.

The old man rocked and cradled Erik in his arms for a moment, and then his eyes opened and set squarely on mine. He said in a firm, commanding voice, "You take care of this baby." And somehow I managed "I will" from a throat that contained a stone. He pried Erik from his chest, unwillingly, longingly, as though he was in pain. I held my arms open to receive my baby, and again the gentleman addressed me: "God bless you, Ma'am. You've given me my Christmas gift." I said nothing more than a muttered "thanks." With Erik in my arms, I ran for the car. Dennis wondered why I was crying and holding Erik so tightly. And why I was saying, "My God, forgive me. Forgive me."

I would like to suggest that the real meaning of Christmas is in this story. Simply put, Erik is God. Simply put, the bum is us. Erik is God's yearning and passion for us tattered bums with our tattered lives, our tattered hurts, our tattered relationships, and our tattered sins. Erik is two arms determined to hug us. Erik is a fierce little baby who makes no distinctions but would embrace the least likely—you and me.

"And the Word became flesh and lived among us" (Jn 1:14).

That's what Christmas is about. It's an enormously unrelenting kind of a feast. It is not sentimentality. It is not soft. It is not sweet baby Jesus. Christmas is volatile Erik. When you look at the manger, there is no cooing baby here: only love satisfied. This is why, when you come right down to it, we celebrate Christmas. If God is not with us and if God has not embraced our tattered lives, woe is us. There is no hope. And there is no light, only darkness and despair.

Most likely, we are here today because of our fruitless socializing, our pressured routine, or our empty sentimentality. But if we are here because of love and we are here like the rag tag shepherds that we are, to kneel and rejoice at the birth of Jesus, then we have caught the meaning of Christmas: Emmanuel, the passionate God, has had his way and has hugged us fiercely.

God's Outreach

So revelation is Erik. Revelation is God's outreach. It deals with a (passionate) Person, not a proposition, and—this is important—such revelation came to us first by way of story, a told story, an oral story. Story is the first revelation, and the oral stories have been around for a long, long time. As we shall see, in accord with human nature, the stories were expanded, embellished, and recast through time, space, and various cultures. It couldn't be otherwise if they were to stay alive.

But by and by, people began to write down these stories in order that they might not be lost. And, of course, the same human tendency developed: the written stories themselves were reworked so that people of different times and places could benefit from them. After all, you couldn't tell a story about a clever polar bear to people in South Africa who had never seen one or heard of one, and so you might have to change the polar bear to a fox or a lion in order to preserve your point.

But then something happened to all this oral stories that had been retold and recast in writing. Sooner or later, someone decided that certain stories that had been written down should become definitive and official and that no other versions would be tolerated. Or if certain other versions of the stories were tolerated because they had valuable insights, they would still be subservient to the official writings. In one way, this was necessary so that the stories wouldn't become distorted, especially by people who had axes to grind, and wouldn't lead people astray.

And so it was. A canon was formed, a norm: these and these books alone are declared official, the standard by which all other teachings and stories and books were to be measured. This process was indeed helpful; but it had some unfortunate, unforeseen side effects. For one thing, the written text, unlike the volatile story, became frozen. And so we need interpreters to clear up the polar bear/fox sort of thing.

Secondly, the official interpreters, now people of standing (the scribes and the Pharisees or the theologians and bishops), tended to over-protect the written text. These guardians became somewhat absolute in their stance and people had to conform to their inscribed pronouncements. Insights from cultural and tradition as well as religious folklore were barely tolerated. The interpreters set lots of rules for understanding and believing (faith), and derivative rules for acting (morals). Sometimes these rules also became so frozen and rigid that God's freely given Self-disclosure was clouded over because there were so many hoops to jump through in order to get to it. That must have made God frustrated many times. The following story tells us what sometimes happened.

> One evening a workman was wearily plodding home when he stopped to rest by the side of the road. A woman came by hauling a cart full of flowers. The smell of her blossoms so perfumed the air with sweetness that it seemed to take away the weariness in his bones and to lighten his spirits. He had

never experienced such wonder from the many blooms of his own garden.

"How much must I pay, or what must I do, to have some of your wonderful flowers?" he asked the woman. "Oh, good sir," she said, "take what you wish." "What return must I make for them?" he questioned again. "Your gratitude is enough," she said. So the man filled his arms with blossoms and hastened joyfully home. And his wife and his children rejoiced with him over the remarkable flowers, for they, too, discovered that the sight of the was a delight and the smell of them refreshed the soul.

So as not to lose his treasure, the man planted the blossoms in a small plot of land behind his house. Sunlight and water kept them amazingly beautiful, still performing their marvelous magic. When children came to play in the yard, the man cautioned them against carelessness and wild play lest they trample the flowers and damage them. But the flowers remained hardy and strong so long as there was enough sun and moisture to nourish them.

Nowhere else could the man or his wife or children find such remarkable solace from weariness, such comfort in sadness, such spiritual nourishment as those remarkable flowers provided. Here was a treasure beyond value.

And as the family grew and more children came to play in the garden, the man became even more concerned over his remarkable flowers. He was determined to protect them, and so he built a high wall around them. In time, because of his numerous children, he would allow them entrance to the small sanctuary only sparingly and with the utmost care. Unfortunately, this began to cause consternation among the family members. If the children caused their father stress or anguish, he would refuse them access to the flowers. Eventually he set up rules as to who might enter the sanctuary, how they must enter, and what they must do while they were in there. For his part he continued to see that his treas-

ure received enough sunlight and water so that the flowers
continued to perform their wondrous magic

As grandchildren began to appear, the man felt even
greater need to safeguard his treasure. Access to the flowers
was open to all members of his family, but not without certain precautions. Requirements were to be met and standards upheld. Offices were established to judge worthiness
and to determine accessibility. It became necessary to have
lawyers to defend and judges to weigh and guards to stand
guard and caretakers to upkeep, and on and on and on. The
man's family, however, saw less and less of the flowers and
experienced less and less of their magical powers.

In the meantime, many of them went out in search of the
flower lady. Well, she was still out there, still giving away her
amazing flowers. (John Aurelio, *Colors!*).

I think we can all resonate with this story. The freely given gifts
of the old lady (God) sometimes became constricted with rigid
rules made by well-meaning caretakers. Too often, the official
interpretation became more important than the text, and the text
became more important than the One behind it.

2.

TIME MARCHES ON

So now we have "official" stories in "official" books. But time marches on, and in due time, as people became more literate, they forgot they were reading imaginative stories that were trying to express the inexpressible, and they began reading the text literally: what it said was what it was. Metaphors, figures of speech, story adjustments, and so on, were literalized. For example, if the text said that God created the world in six days, then six days it was. If the text reported that the whale swallowed Jonah whole (how he escaped the teeth and digestive juices of the whale was never discussed!), then that's what happened. If the text said that Joshua blew down the walls of Jericho by blasts of the trumpets, then those scientists who demonstrate that the walls were already down three hundred years before Joshua were wrong. If Matthew gorgeously recounts that wise men came from the East, then they did. We became so enamored with the written text that we no longer looked behind it to the stories that gave rise to the text—not to mention looking behind the story to the Storyteller!

Since people forgot they were basically reading oral stories they applied literary rules to the biblical text, rather than story-telling rules, which are totally different. This put people into all kinds of serious and silly conundrums. More seriously, as we shall soon explore, people (mostly the elite leaders) not only made the fixed text sacrosanct but they themselves almost total-ly forgot the fluid, dynamic stories behind the text. They soon gave idolatrous obedience to what was down on paper, rendering disdain for the story itself. "Truth" was to be found in the text itself, not in the story behind the text.

Finally, people forgot that the original storytellers knew what we all know but have been brainwashed by print to ignore: truth is always more compatible and digestible in story form than in print form. An old eighteenth-century tale says it all:

In the beginning of time, Truth walked quite naked upon the Earth. His skin was smooth and shining, his body was strong and well formed, and he walked tall and proud. Everywhere he went, Truth tried to share the great store of knowledge that he possessed and so each time he entered a village, he would cry out loudly, "I am Truth. Come and learn from my teachings."

But I must tell you, surprisingly no one listened to Truth. Oh, yes, sometimes some children came running to sit at his feet and hear him talk, but soon their parents dragged them away, covering the children's eyes with their hands. Sometimes a young woman was drawn to Truth, looking at him with won-der and listening with awe, but her mother immediately repri-manded her and turned her aside. Young men on their part looked at him with envy and fear and turned quickly away. Old women looked at him with fond, reminiscent smiles and old men with a look of chagrin. But still, no one listened and so Truth wandered from village to village, town to town, always with the same reception, and always alone.

Well, one day he found himself in the neighborhood where his sister, Story lived. She lived in a fine and fancy house, surrounded by flowers and ferns, trees, and blossoming vines. A wide, shady porch stretched around the house, filled with comfortable rocking chairs, soft cushions, and hanging swings. The wide windows were hung with lace curtains and brocade drapes, and stained glass cast rainbows of light across the oriental carpets. And there was Story herself sitting in a wide wicker chair, dressed in a flowing chiffon gown that shimmered with light and color. Her curling hair tumbled about her shoulders, and was strewn with flowers and ribbons, and her fingers and throat, wrists and ankles were adorned with jewels.

When Story saw her brother approaching, she got up and ran to him, but she stopped and put her hands to her face. She cried out, "Why, Truth, dear brother, you look awful. You look so sad and dejected. What's wrong? How can I help you?" "I don't think anyone can help me, Story," said Truth. "I've gone to every village and town, trying to share my knowledge, and no one will listen. I have such important things to say, Story! But I can't make them listen!" "You're wrong, my Brother. I can help you. I know just what you need. Come with me."

So Story led Truth into her bedroom, where she threw open trunks and hampers and armoires full of clothes, shoes, hats, and cloaks. "Dress yourself, Truth. Dress yourself up!" Truth was horrified and shrank back. "Dress myself up? Dress myself up in these gaudy things? Oh, no, Story, I can't! I really can't. I'd feel so silly." But Story insisted and insisted, and finally Truth gave in. He put on purple trousers made of velvet, a fine linen shirt with billowing sleeves, and a quilted vest sewn with glittering jewels. He wrapped a flowing silken scarf around his neck, and hung golden hoops from his ears. He put rings on every finger, a pair of silver shoes on his feet, and on his head he wore a hat with a long curving feather. When he thought he was finished, Story wove ribbons into his hair, poked a flower into his lapel, and hung a satin cloak around his shoulders.

Story stood back and looked at her brother. At last she was satisfied. "Now you are ready, " she told him. "Go back to the villages, and see what happens. " Truth felt quite ridiculous, but he thanked Story and set out once more to enlighten the World. After one year, he returned to Story's house. "What happened, Truth?" She asked "You look much happier than the last time I saw you. Truth was ectatic. "I really don't understand it, Story, but these silly clothes worked! Everywhere I went, people would gather around and listen eagerly to everything I had to say! It was wonderful, but I'm confused. I still have the same things to say. Why will people listen now to what they rejected before? Story replied, "Don't you see? No one wants to listen to the naked Truth, but everyone will listen when it's clothed in Story."

That's what the biblical writers thought too when they collected the stories of a loving God. Because less than two percent of the ancient world could read, reading Scripture was always interactive. That is to say, the rare person who could read would read aloud to a large crowd. He would read with meaning, gesture, and interpretation and in response the audience would shout (like some African-American assemblies who pepper "Amens" throughout the preacher's sermon) and "ohh" and "ahh." Even though the stories had been written down, the revelation, or communication, of God through interactive stories remained largely intact. Truth, as it should, became all gussied up in the biblical stories. Try this truth-in-story:

After an attack on a synagogue, the rabbi was asked to make charges against the perpetrators. He refused. The police told him that if he did nothing, then more attacks could happen. Did he want that? "No", he replied, "but even less do I want to call attention to ourselves. We've been through this before in other countries. It seems best to choose the quieter course."

When challenged again, the rabbi—what else?—told a story. He said, "Once there was a great forest and it had many wolves. They made themselves known every night by their howling, to the moon, to one another. Then one year the nobles of the district could stand the clamor no longer. They organized a hunting party and finally all the wolves were killed. There was no more howling. Now there were foxes in the forest too. The fox indeed is a very shy animal, very quiet. And there are foxes in that forest still today."

Modern Subversion

As strangers to the oral-storytelling tradition, we moderns are stuck almost exclusively with the written record, the Bible. Consequently we often find it a most difficult book to read and understand. No wonder many of us have never read it. It was written and compiled over a thousand years in languages we don't know (some passages in the ancient languages still baffle even the scholars), in a culture far removed from us, with examples and metaphors we no longer grasp. Entering the biblical world is like entering Middle Earth for the first time and trying to adjust to the elvish languages, hobbits, wizards, and strange terrains: we're completely disoriented.

And because we have read the Bible literally for so many centuries, we are easily shocked and scandalized when we hear that, because of modern scholarship, such a literal reading doesn't hold water anymore. Eager publishers with an eye to sales tell us so loudly and clearly in their many books. National magazines like *Newsweek, Time, US News & World Report*, and so on, regularly undermine cherished beliefs. Novels come along to tell us that Jesus was married to Mary Magdalene and they had a child and that all this "truth," was, of course, suppressed by a wicked Church full of self-serving bureaucrats. Archaeologists, scholars, pundits, and other talking heads routinely appear on TV at Christmas and Easter to instruct us that, for example, there is no archaeological evidence that the Exodus ever took place, that Abraham, Isaac, Jacob, and Moses are mythical figures like King Arthur, and that the names of the twelve tribes of Israel are never the same.

Yes, the walls that Joshua was supposed to have toppled with a blast of his trumpets actually were destroyed three hundred years before his time. There are two versions of the death of Saul in the Bible; also, the giant Goliath was slain by David in one place and by Elhanan in another. Moreover, modern scholars declare, we really don't know who wrote the gospels—certainly it was not the names of Matthew, Mark, Luke, and John that were attached to these gospels a hundred and fifty years or so after they were written. And, oh yes, scholars are fond of reminding us that Jesus was really born at Nazareth, not Bethlehem, and that there were no magi, star, or shepherds there. Peter quotes words from the Old Testament that are not to be found anywhere in Scripture; the gospels give two different versions of the Our Father, and four different versions of the simple words over the cross. Indeed, discrepancies abound. And not to add fuel to the fire, but

1. that's only the beginning, and
2. the scholars are right.

If you are upset to find this out—and rightly so—it's because of the way you and I have been trained to hear or read the Bible; that is, literally. We come at it from a literary, printed point of view, and as a result, we are upset by all the contradictions and versions and episodes that don't make sense.

So in this small book, I want to give you a key to how to read the Bible—or listen to it at Mass or in study groups. The approach I am going to explore with you—in case you didn't read the introduction—the framework we will use to throw light on most of the biblical issues is, of course, storytelling. I'm in good company: "Jesus told the crowds all these things in parables; without a parable he told them nothing" (Mt 13:34).

3.

A Library
of Stories

Remember that the Bible is an anthology, a collection of stories. Some of these are very old—like Miriam's song in Exodus 15, which dates back perhaps to 1200 BC—and other stories are from as early as 400 BC, such as the book of Daniel. Not only that, but sometimes, this widely spread-out story material gets patched together with no explanation. For example, Genesis 2:4a and Genesis 2:4b patches together material from the ninth and the fourth centuries BC. Again, the Bible is an anthology covering material from a span of over 1000 years that has been collected under one cover. That's why it's really not right to generalize and say, "The Bible says…," because it makes a difference if you're quoting from an historical book like Kings or a fiction novella like the Jonah or poetry such as the psalms.

It's like going to the library. Yes, it's one building, but it has a history section, a literature section, a science section, a poetry section, a mystery section, a fiction section, a biography section, and so on. When we go to a library, you and I adjust our minds and expectations to the shelf and section we choose. In other words, we don't expect objective statements from poetry or history from science fiction. If I'm reading an Agatha Christie murder mystery with Hercule Poirot, I'm not reading it the same way or with the same assumptions as I would were I reading Grandpa's last will and testament. So, why should all seventy-two books of the Bible say the same thing in the same way? Yet that's what people expect.

I was reading about a man who was flying from Des Moines to San Francisco. In the course of the flight he chatted with his seat companion who, he found out, was a flat-Earther; that is, the man did not believe that the world was round. When asked why, the man replied, "It says in the book of Revelation that the angels will stand in the four corners of the earth. The earth couldn't have four corners if it was round."

Talk about a classic case of the literal mind at work! The man thought the Book of Revelation was a science book that taught cosmology and he read it that way. But, of course, it's not. It's a piece of highly imaginative and figurative literature called "apocalyptic," a kind of psychedelic, strobe-light writing that teaches theology. In the passage the man quoted (7:1) the author of Revelation is simply indicating, in a nice bit of imagery, that angels would come from all points of the compass. In any case, we have in the Bible "Truth clothed in Story." Therefore, what I am saying is that we ought to apply the same criteria to this biblical story collection as we apply to all stories.

The Bible as Narrative
To put it simply, we are challenged to engage the Bible as narrative, as story, and (as we shall see shortly) to be aware of the reader's response or involvement in the text. The Bible, I must repeat, is a compendium of stories, laws, hymns, proverbs, poems, letters, and visions that are timely and unforgettable. Tom Winton, a prize-winning author who is one of Australia's most popular

writers, was asked about the Protestant church he attended in his youth and what grabbed his imagination there. He replied:

> When I look back I see two things. One is the complete lack of any intellectual life in that church community. I see a complete aridity of the physical and sensual life of the church. But I do remember the richness of the life of story that came out of that. The storyness of Scripture, its narrative nature, appealed to me instantly (*Image*, Summer 1995).

On the Catholic side, Andrew Greeley maintains that story—meaning the biblical stories and their spinoffs—is the reason why Catholics stay in the church. He says that it's the poetic, metaphorical, and ritual dimensions of our faith that are so captivating and possessing:

> Because we are reflective creatures we must also reflect on our religious experiences and stories; it is in the (lifelong) interlude of reflection that propositional religion and religious authority become important, indeed indispensable. But then the religiously mature person returns to the imagery, having criticized it, analyzed it, questioned it, to commit the self once more in sophisticated and reflective maturity to the story....If you want to understand Catholics—and if Catholics want to understand themselves—the starting point is to comprehend the enormous appeal of that [religious] sensibility. It's the stories. (*New York Times Magazine*, 7/10/94).

Thomas Long expresses it this way:

> The odd thing about biblical stories is that there are so many of them. There are battle stories, betrayal stories, stories about seduction and treachery in the royal court, stories about farmers and fools, healing stories, violent stories, funny stories and sad ones, stories of death, and stories of resurrection the claim that the Bible is a "story book" is not far off the mark. (*Preaching and the Literary Fonts of the Bible*).

So if the Bible is indeed a storybook, as these writers all state, then we should treat it as such.

Some Storytelling Principles

The first principle to note is that stories are incredibly important and formative. If we are what we eat, then even more so, we are the stories we know, cherish, and live by. Our formative stories start early. The ones told by our parents, teachers, and friends stick with us.

Story is used in therapy. Psychologists have found that people prefer stories over facts and lists of information. We are hard-wired to listen to and tell stories. As one writer reports:

A recent issue of the *Harvard Business Review* (June 2003) features an interview with a screenwriting coach who explains why executives need to understand and employ narrative; "Forget about Power Point and statistics. To involve people at the deepest level, you need stories. Stories are how we remember; we tend to forget lists and bullet points." An article in the *New York Times* (June 23, 2003) explains that many entertainment producers attribute the success of their most highly rated new shows to "solid stories and concepts," often made with lesser-known actors, rather than the star power of expensive celebrities.

Even science is embracing the story: a new field in medicine has emerged called narrative medicine. Under the direction of Rita Charon, a physician and literature PhD, Columbia University's College of Physicians and Surgeons now offers a program in this field, which their Web site defines as "medicine practiced with narrative competence." An explanation of the program states that "When doctors can recognize, absorb, interpret, and be moved to action by the narratives of their patients, they can practice a medicine marked by empathy, accuracy, and effectiveness."

None of this should be news to us, of course. The Christian tradition, as well as many other religious traditions, is rich in storytelling. Christ didn't give theological lectures so as much as he told stories....More than anything, stories give us a window through which to understand life and why it changes. We have a powerful need to be part of a story larger than ourselves. Psychologist and author William K. Kilpatrick, in his book *Why Johnny Can't Tell Right from Wrong*, explains it this way: "The same impulse that makes us want our books to have a plot makes us want our lives to have a plot. We need to feel that we are getting somewhere, making progress...." Kilpatrick also warns about what happens when the narrative sense is missing from individual lives, stating, "Both for society and the individual the loss of story and history amounts to a loss of memory. We become amnesiacs, not knowing where we are going, because we don't know where we have come from." (Sarah Koops Vanderveen, editor's note in an article entitled "Storytelling" in the *Mars Hill Review*, issue 22, 2003).

If we look around us, we see a lot of glitzy, shallow, rootless people who are living only for the moment. At the bottom they are story-less as they live by the hollow manufactured stories of a commercial media which has taught them, with great effectiveness, that they are what they possess, consume, or display. To change the metaphor, with no foundational stories, they are all flashy book jackets with no contents inside. Note the obsessive concern with image among both women and men; cosmetic surgery is not far and away the nation's most frequently performed operation for nothing.

As we shall have occasion to mention frequently, the Bible, both the Old and New Testaments, are fundamentally story books and these stories provoke, challenge, and reveal. So that's our first principle in approaching the Bible: the stories are formative. They are who we are. And we are only doing what is natural when we read the Bible to discover who we are.

The second principle to remember is this: that biblical stories, like all ancestral stories, were first told. That sounds like a no-brainer, something so obvious we don't often think about it, and as a disastrous result, interpreting these stories from a scribal mindset rather than from an imaginative mindset. But the fact is the Bible stories, lore, epics, and poetry were told long, long before they found their way into writing, into literature. And therefore they follow, as we shall see, all the rules of oral storytelling and not the rules of written grammar and composition; that makes a huge difference.

If we don't apply oral rules to the Bible (which, sadly, we seldom do) but apply the canons of the later written text, then it will be difficult, if not impossible, to come to terms with the many contradictions in the Bible. Worse, we fall into the intractable and besetting sin that has caused, and still causes, so much difficulty: taking the printed Bible literally and creating fixed doctrines out of fluid stories. This is as futile as trying "to hold a moonbeam in your hand," as Mother Superior sang in *The Sound of Music.*

4.

HURTFUL
PREJUDICE

To appreciate the power, fluidity, and truth-telling power of the oral story, we must do some serious head work. This is quite demanding, but hang in there. We must first overcome two strong cultural prejudices which we all unconsciously carry around. The first is our unconscious belief in the superiority of the written over the storied word, that truth is in the former but not the latter. The second is the profound cultural gap, almost a chasm, between us modern-day Westerners and the Mediterraneans of biblical times.

Let's look at the first cultural prejudice. Why do we revere the written word over the spoken word? (Why is there no great oratory any more?) Because that's the way we have been raised over the past three hundred years. And today, that prejudice is more than ever ingrained in us because, in our society, we are almost totally immersed in print. Even the ubiquitous television reporters and talking heads are nothing more than a spoken script. So conditioned are we that, in our minds, the mighty printed word—be it newspaper, book, report, document, or Power Point presentation—is the criterion for what is real and valid. A story? Well, it's just that: a story, or worse, a myth, a fanciful concoction. How could we get to know any kind of truth, say, from a fairy tale like Jack in the Beanstalk or that ridiculous story some Jewish rabbi told of the prodigal son? A story told versus the page printed: for us there is no contest.

But step back and think: the printed word, literature itself, is very new on the human scene. For most of human existence, people were illiterate—in some places on the globe, they still are. (Illiterate means that someone cannot read, *not* that he or she is not intelligent, or cannot speak, or tell or know the truth.) Besides that, remember another thing: human consciousness is first oral. As scholar Walter Ong says,

> It is the oral word that first illuminates consciousness with articulate language, that first divides subject and predicate and then relates them to one another, and that ties human beings to one another in society.

In other words, each of us is born into a world that is at first totally oral and aural, consisting of the spoken word and the heard word. Fetal research has proven this, by demonstrating that our first experiences of the world are oral-aural, and begin even before we are born. It has been shown, in fact, that as newborns in the delivery room we are able to distinguish our mother's voice from all the other noises coming at us. Sound guides sight as the infant's unfocused eyes track and follow that sound until a visual oral-aural association is made.

The oral-aural relationship, then—the speaking-listening relationship and all of its dynamics, also known as "storying"—is arguably one of the oldest and most elemental forms of knowing. I use the phrase, "and all of its dynamics" because the oral-aural word, unlike the printed word, is always flexible, poised for nuance and changing circumstances. Which is to say that stories, unlike print, are fluid. Tell the exact same story a moment later to the same group of people and an entirely different story may very well be heard, for no two oral performances by a single person are ever the same. In other words, meaning, significance, and impact may be very similar from telling to telling, but they will never be identical (we'll see that when we look at some Scripture passages).

In spoken form the word is repeated, expanded, and transformed every time it is used. In written form, the word can be frozen, made static, invariable, or even petrified. Once written, the word can only be changed with difficulty (remember Pontius Pilate's words, "What I have written, I have written" in John 19:22?). With storying, however, truth refuses to be pinned down, reduced, or equated with any particular form or formula or text. That is because there is always more truth. It is worth noting that oral cultures—the majority of the world—have no dictionaries. Why? Because, as I just wrote, the meaning of each word is controlled by the real-life situations in which the word is used here and now. If the English teacher today told his class that they were going to read Noel Coward's play, "The Gay Divorcée," the students would smile knowingly and whisper "no wonder they got divorced!"

You see, words acquire their meaning from current context, and from social signals such as gestures, cultural assumptions, vocal inflections, facial expressions, and the human, existential setting in which the real, spoken word always occurs. (There is, for example, a dictionary that interprets Italian gestures.) That's one reason why we have so much trouble with the Bible stories. We tend to read them with our printed word mindsets, as fixed, inscribed words, and thus we find some of the stories horrifying or obtuse. But biblical stories must be read and understood not only in their ancient Mediterranean cultural context, but also in their ancient oral context, not in our contemporary scribal context. And so the key to reading Scripture should always consider *not* what is set down in type but what is meant in sound. Reading the stories of the Bible cannot be done with an attitude of "what does it say?" but with an oral attitude that asks, "what does the story, however weird or fantastic, mean?"

The Tyranny of Print

We're so ingrained with a literate-scribal mentality that I must once again hammer home my point. Look at it this way: every-thing—everything—started out with sound, from science to for-mal religion. It was around the campfire on a starry night that the first astronomers wondered aloud about the movement of the planets. Storying existed in the old Mesopotamian and Babylonian flood tales which were retold and adopted and adapted over the years by Hebrew storytellers. Finally—much, much later—these stories were written down, just as were the *Iliad* and the *Odyssey* of Homer and the legends of King Arthur. All of these had a long, long history of oral telling and endless adaptations before being put down on a stone, parchment, or page. The fact is, long before the alphabet, long before writing—which occurred very late in human history—story was the way that one came to know reality in all its phases and ambiguities.

Now enter the villain. In the years after Gutenberg invented the printing press, oral-aural storying began to seem embarrassingly crude compared to the linear precision, dependable efficiency, and uniform organization of print, especially to the elite classes who were exposed to the written word. Orally-based thought and expression was soon considered "primitive," "savage," "inferior," "coarse," or "despicable." Among the poor, the disenfranchised, the dispossessed, and all those without access to education and literacy, oral-aural storying persisted but—again, in the eyes of the elite—as a devalued currency.

Storytelling was soon categorized as a tool of the illiterate, and illiteracy came to be synonymous with stupidity. (The ancient sages like Socrates would be amused at such arrogance.) The result was that only those who could read and write were consid-ered educated—a sentiment that continues to today—just as only the printed word has been considered worthy of the name "liter-ature." Uncle Remus, for example, would be considered a rube, unlettered, and ignorant.

In the last three hundred years, with the rise of the so-called "modern" scientific method in the seventeenth century, there has occurred a shift from the preeminence of story to the dominance of science, a shift that has defined the advent of the modern mind. Story as a genuine and more true way of knowing reality gradually came to be considered an inferior remnant of a "premodern" consciousness, a "backward" kind of thinking, a primitive entertainment fit only for children, the illiterate, and the uneducated. Why, we even say to our kids, "You're telling a story, aren't you?" when we catch them in a lie, thereby showing how far story has declined.

The tyranny escalated. Literacy—being able to read and write and manipulate the written word (now easily done by computer)—became quite imperious in time. It tended to consider itself as normative for human expression, thought, and truth. No more tall tales from Grandma's lap, tales that made you think or ponder. No, forget that nonsense. The new snobbish tyranny was this: nothing is true unless it is written down on paper. Thus, as night follows day, bureaucracy was born. After all, in an exclusively paper-print world, there must be, has to be, a supervisory class of people who will oversee human procedures and who will decide how to translate human experience into languages and categories and codes that are simple and convenient for purposes of record keeping, surveillance, and evaluation.

So, little by little, by developing rules, quotas, printed forms, spreadsheets, statistics, copying machines, filing cabinets, and data bases, a whole new technology has been established for knowing, experiencing, and relating to self, other, and the world. (Think of the ubiquitous cellphone, which substitutes for face to face conversation.) In this, our time, you and I are immersed in real or electronic paper. You can't buy a house, apply to college, drive a car, add on a room, seek a credit card, get medical attention, go to court, or even die without reams and reams of documents and affidavits. Our lives are dominated by paperwork and by those who translate and mediate it; that is, the lawyers. That's why we have so many of them.

Well, the irony is that, in time, the world transcribed on paper became even more important and of greater concern than the world of human experience, so much so that, if no record of an event, meeting, or encounter can be produced then, in the world of bureaucracy, it could never have happened—no matter how many people say it did. If it's not written down somewhere, it doesn't exist; if there are no permanent records of people in a bureaucratic system, they never existed—until records can be generated for them. Things are not true unless recorded. That's the world we live in and that's why it's hard to appreciate the power and truthfulness of verbal stories—especially the biblical stories with all of the contradictions, exaggerations, and expansions that naturally go into oral storytelling.

Scientism

And so today's cultural problem with the Bible and all ancient writings is our dearly held assumption that all knowledge must be scientifically verifiable. Every modern person believes this way. Knowledge, "real" knowledge, must be observed and measured, capable of being plugged into a data base. That's its validation. It's like the large print on the outside of a product that shouts, "As seen on television!" You can't get a better validation than that in our media age.

This kind of thinking is called "scientism." In this system, value judgements about the good, the beautiful, or the true are not considered "real" knowledge, just somebody's subjective feelings. Spreadsheets, data put down in black and white—now there's knowledge and truth. Poetry, legends, fairy tales, and stories don't cut it. Science, you see, is deductive and cerebral. Wisdom is inductive and imaginative.

Is one better than the other in our search for meaning? Not at all. In fact, we claim, as the biblical writers implicitly do, that this deductive, imaginative way of wisdom is indeed an avenue to truth. We claim that poets and painters know something important about birds and plants that ornithologists and botanists might miss. As an example of such wisdom here is Robert Browning Hamilton's oft-quoted poem:

> I walked a mile with Pleasure;
> She chatted all the way.
> But left me none the wiser
> For all she had to say.
>
> I walked a mile with Sorrow
> And ne'er a word said she;
> But, oh, the things I learned from her
> When Sorrow walked with me!

That's not far from the words of St. Augustine: "And where was I to find such pleasures save in you, O Lord, You who use sorrow now to teach, and wound us to heal, and kill us lest we die to you?" (*Confessions*, 2.2.) Is there no deep truth in the imageries here? How about Leigh Hunt's delight:

> Abou Ben Adhem (may his tribe increase!)
> Awoke one night from a deep dream of peace,
> And saw, within the moonlight in his room,
> Making it rich, and like a lily in bloom
>
> An Angel writing in a book of gold:
> Exceeding peace had made Ben Adhem bold,
> And to the Presence in the room he said,
> "What writest thou?" The Vision raised its head,
>
> And with a look made of all sweet accord
> Answered, "The names of those who love the Lord."
> "And is mine one?" said Abou. "Nay, not so,"
> Replied the Angel. Abou spoke more low
>
> But cheerily still; and said, "I pray thee, then
> Write me as one that loves his fellow men."
> The Angel wrote, and vanished. The next night
> It came again with a great wakening light,
> And showed the names whom love of God had blessed,

And, lo! Ben Adhem's name led all the rest!

This poem echoes Jesus' words: "Not everyone who says to me, 'Lord, Lord,' will enter the kingdom of heaven, but only the one who does the will of my Father in heaven" (Mt 7:21). Angels, dreams, lilies in bloom, a book of gold—this is not exactly the stuff of objective, scientific data. Yet are these figures of the imagination any less real? Is the poem's message suspect for playing around with words and images? Do the fictional works of Dante Alighieri, William Shakespeare, Fyodor Dostoevsky, Jane Austen, Charles Dickens, John Cheever, Graham Greene, Flannery O'Connor, Edith Wharton, and others like them have no wisdom, no truth, to teach us? Do the brutal stories in the Book of Judges, the fiction in the Book of Jonah, the wild, off-the-wall images in the Book of Revelation have nothing to say to us? The scientific mentality is impatient with all of this and declares it impossible and contradictory and false. The imaginative mentality, on the other hand, recognizes and relishes in these literary and biblical books what cannot be measured or blatantly expressed.

The scholar Robert Alter is on to something when he remarks that, until the parables of Kafka or James Joyce's *Ulysses* came along, modern people had lost the skills necessary to read the Bible precisely because we had lost the ability to see through the images. Only after artists were determined to transcribe reality on a number of levels (not just the "scientific"), he says, exploring the complexities of human consciousness, the mystery of time, the polyvalence of words, were we able to ask the right questions of the Bible. And that is what this book is all about: to search out the oral, imaged truth behind the literal words, to learn to read the Bible, not as an objective text written by modern Americans, but as a storybook written by a storytelling people of old.

No less than that profound pagan, D.H. Lawrence, agrees with Alter and urges us to become "untamed" by

listening in to the voices of the honourable beasts that call
in the dark paths of the veins of our body, from the God in

the heart. Listening inwards, inwards, not for words nor for inspiration, but to the lowing of the innermost beasts, the feelings that roam in the forest of the blood, from the feet of God within the red, dark heart.

With his words in mind, read Geoffrey Hill's poem, *Lachrimae Amantis*:

> What is there in my heart that you should sue
> so fiercely for its love? What kind of care
> brings you as though a stranger to my door
> through the long night and in the icy dew
> seeking the heart that will not harbor you,
> that keeps itself religiously secure?
>
> At this dark solstice filled with frost and fire
> your passion's ancient wounds must bleed anew.
>
> So many nights the angel of my house
> has fed such urgent comfort through a dream,
> whispered "your lord is coming, he is close"
> that I have drowsed half-faithful for a time
> bathed in pure tones of promise and remorse:
> "tomorrow I shall wake to welcome him."
>
> *New & Collected Poems: 1952-1992*

Heart, door, dark solstice, dreams, tones of promise—hard to pinpoint or analyze or get down on paper but, deep down, these images speak truth to us in language Augustine would recognize, he who prayed daily for chastity to come—but "tomorrow."

We have a mindset. It's a very recent one, only some three or four hundred years old. It's a mindset that says science is the measurement of all objective truth. At least that is the official stance enshrined in our political and educational systems.

Unofficially, the wildly popular *Lord of the Rings*, the Harry Potter series, and other fantasy productions testify to our subconscious roots, our ancient resonance, our human need to seek the Other who can be encountered but not captured.

5.

Oral Story vs. Print

A man walks into a restaurant with a full-grown ostrich behind him. As they sit at a table, the waitress comes over and asks for their orders. The man looks over the menu and says, "I'll have a hamburger, fries, and a coke," and turns to the ostrich, "What's yours?" "I'll have the same," says the ostrich. A short time later the waitress returns with the order. "That will be $5.84 please," and the man reaches into his pocket and pulls out the exact change for payment.

The next day, the man and the ostrich come again and the man says, "I'll have a hamburger, fries, and a coke," and the ostrich says, "I'll have the same." Once again the man reaches into his pocket and pays with exact change. This becomes a routine until late one evening, the two enter again. "The usual?" asks the waitress. "No," the man pauses, "this is

Saturday night, so I tell you what. I'll have a steak, baked potato and salad." "Same for me," says the ostrich.

A short time later the waitress comes with the order and says, "That will be $23.65." Once again the man pulls exact change out of his pocket and places it on the table. The waitress can't hold back her curiosity any longer. "Excuse me, sir. How do you manage to always come up with the exact change out of your pocket every time?"

"Well," says the man, "several years ago I was cleaning the attic and I found an old lamp. When I rubbed it a genie appeared and offered me two wishes. My first wish was that if I ever had to pay for anything, I would just put my hand in my pocket and the right amount of money would always be there."

"That's brilliant!" says the waitress. "Most people would wish for a million dollars or something, but you'll always be as rich as you want for as long as you live!"

"That's right," replied the man. "Whether it's a gallon of milk or a Rolls Royce the exact money is always there."

The waitress asks, "One other thing, sir, what's with the ostrich?" The man sighs, pauses, and answers, "My second wish was for a tall chick with long legs who agrees with everything I say."

That's a funny joke. We accept it on its own terms and let out a guffaw. But I'm going to do something that no one should ever, ever do with a joke: analyze it. To analyze a joke is to kill it; but in the interest of this chapter, allow me to commit some literary homicide.

There are three things going on here, so subtle that we do not even realize it. First, the joke is a narrative. We listen to it because that's the kind of people we are. We are wired for narrative. We always want to know what's coming next. A good story or a good movie grab us. We ourselves are a narrative with a beginning, middle, and end. We are part of a larger story, whether it be blind evolution or a divine plan. We listen because narratives—even a silly joke—are innately compelling.

Second, notice how we suspend judgment.

For one thing, you have an ostrich walking into a restaurant; for another, the bird talks. If you're telling the joke, and when you come to the part where the ostrich says, "I'll have the same" someone interrupts you and says, "Wait a minute! Hold it! Ostriches don't talk" and proceeds to make a big fuss over the point, you would probably strangle the clod and no jury would convict you; he's missed the point. He is what we call a "fundamentalist," and fundamentalists come in both Protestant and Catholic versions. Strictly speaking, the man's right, of course: ostriches don't talk. We all know that, but the average person takes the story on its own terms and sees what it has to say even if it goes against logic and knowledge. We let the illogical slide in the interest of the punch line.

Third, besides the sheer fun of the joke, you can even get serious (which you shouldn't do) and draw a moral lesson from it, a "truth dressed in story" kind of thing. For example, "Be careful what you wish for."

All this is meant to focus on a truth we shall serve up in many ways throughout this book: take the story or the type of biblical book (genre) on its own terms whether it's poetry, fiction, theological history, biography, or other. Don't stumble over what seems illogical from our two-to-three thousand-years-later perspective, and our three-hundred-year-old scientific mindset. Don't interrupt and say, donkeys don't talk (as they do in the book of Deuteronomy), or angels don't appear (as they do in Luke), or a temple veil doesn't tear down the middle when someone dies (as it does in Matthew). As in the joke, you have to suspend judgment and focus on the point, the message, the revelation. Don't be a fundamentalist.

The Most Beautiful Lady

So, with that being said, let's move on and take a quick look at some examples of story versus print:

Once upon a time two monks were traveling together down

a muddy road. A heavy rain was still falling. Coming around a bend, they met a lovely girl in a silk kimono and sash, unable to cross the intersection. "Come on, girl," said the first monk at once. Lifting her in his arms, he carried her over the mud. The second monk did not speak until that night, when they reached a lodging temple. Then he could no longer restrain himself. "We monks don't go near females," he told the first monk, "especially not young and lovely ones. It is dangerous. Why did you do that?" "I left the girl there," said the first monk. "Are you still carrying her?"

Is this story factual? Can you produce a transcript of the encounter, sealed and certified? No. Is it true? Does it reflect a truth? What do you think?

Or try this: someone once asked Jesus, who is my neighbor? Today, with modern technology (and the death of privacy), you could get a printout telling you all about your neighbor: his income, marriages, cars, place of employment, where he's lived before, where his children go school, his credit cards, hobbies, the magazines he subscribes to, the papers he reads, and the Websites he visits on his computer. It's all there: my neighbor in a nutshell. (Hi-tech thriller movies like *The Italian Job* or *Enemy of the State* strikingly reveal the disappearance of privacy.)

On the other hand, when asked that same question, the rabbi who never saw a computer print-out, told the story of the Good Samaritan. Is his story factual? No, he made it up out of his head. Is it true? Yes, in ways so varied that you can endlessly revisit this story. You can dwell on the victim, the Samaritan, the Levite, the Jewish priest, the innkeeper, the audience, and even what the original story might have been like before Luke took hold of it. The parable resists any one "valid" interpretation as it challenges the way one lives, or ought to live.

Again: a tearful little boy is telling the police he's lost his mother. "What is she like? Give us a description." "She is the most beautiful lady in the world!" replies the lad. When they do find her she turns out to be a rather mousy, plain woman. She is duly photographed, her vital statistics put into the computer, and now the police know who she is. Or do they? They have a sheet on her but they have no stories about her: of how she stayed up all night to care for her son when he was sick or the surprise birthday party she gave him or the many hugs and kisses that told him he was important and wanted. Where does truth reside when you ask, "What is she like?" Why do we accept the sheet as true but not her story? (This comment belongs to a later chapter, but just remember the boy's words—which are very much in the story-telling biblical mode: exaggerated, "unreal," partisan, unscientific, and subjective, but, oh, so true.) As I wrote in the preface to my book, *More Telling Stories. More Compelling Stories*:

> "Jesus told the crowds all these things in parables; without a parable he told them nothing." Thus reads Matthew's testimony (13:34), whose own infancy narratives show him to be no mean storyteller himself. Come to think of it, there are no lectures recorded from the mouth of Jesus (or pen: he wrote nothing), except those long discourses in that strange last gospel. Jesus obviously was a natural storyteller and those who followed him picked up the habit. True, there were philosophical ruminations from St. Paul on, but the real work of spreading the Good News fell to accounts of Jesus, his disciples, and a whole array of saints. Legends, tales, epics, and myths were the embodiments of deep truths. Stories told of how people actually lived the gospel.
>
> To this day who can forget Jesus as Francis Thompson's "Hound of Heaven," or Francis of Assisi reasoning with the wolf of Gubbio? Who was not tingled to hear Robert Bolt's dialogue between Sir Thomas More and Henry VIII, the former asking the latter why he needed his support when he had everyone else's, and Henry answering, "Because you are honest....There are those like Norfolk who follow me because I wear the crown, and there are those like Master Cromwell who follow me because they are jackals with sharp teeth and I am their lion, and there is a mass that fol-

lows me because it follows anything that moves—and there is you." Who does not see Christ in the life story of a Dorothy Day or Archbishop Romero? The gospel has always been best served by stories, which, after all, came first and then only later the philosophizing, the necessary categories, the systematic theologies.

Are you getting the drift? Oral stories, those products of imagination and creativity, are a source of truth and wisdom that, in many ways, supersedes the written word. As the great Protestant theologian Reinhold Niebuhr put it,

> Fundamentalists have at least one characteristic in common with most scientists. Neither can understand that poetic and religious imagination has a way of arriving at truth by giving a clue to the total meaning of things without being in any sense an analytic description of detailed facts." *(Notebooks)*

Remember that ultimately, there is a story behind all that we know. The Bible is a collection of stories. We know them now as fixed words on a page but for centuries they were told and retold orally-aurally. The truth is in the telling, not in the petrified word. To understand the Bible we must become story-listeners and apply the rules of storytelling to what we hear.

The Subversiveness of Story

There is another reason why oral-aural storying either had to be dismissed as the discourse of the crude, the ignorant, the infantile, and the simple or else "translated" into text-based literature before it could receive "serious" attention from scholars. That reason is this: any recovery of storying as a valid way of knowing would pose a real threat to the "modern" models of objective truth, scientific knowledge, and settled reality that still dominate our world culture today. If that happened too many vested interests would be rattled.

That is because, as I mentioned before, storying challenges the objectivity, control, and permanence that print technology has bequeathed to the modern consciousness. Take this delightful account from a mother who, on at least on this occasion, beat the system. She writes,

> A friend of mine went to the county clerk's office to renew her driver's license. "Do you have a job, or are you just a...?" the recorder asked her. My friend, fuming, snapped: "Of course I have a job. I'm a mother." The recorder replied, "We don't list 'mother' as an occupation. 'Housewife' covers it."
>
> Well, I found myself in the same situation one day when I was at our own town hall. The clerk was obviously a career woman, poised, efficient, and possessed of a high-sounding title, like "Official Interrogator" or "Town Registrar." She asked, "And what is your occupation?" I don't know where they came from, but all of a sudden the words popped out of my mouth: "I'm a Research Associate in the field of Child Development and Human Relations," I said. The clerk paused, pen frozen in midair. I repeated the title slowly: "I'm a Research Associate in the field of Child Development and Human Relations." The clerk wrote my pompous title in bold, black ink on the official questionnaire.
>
> The clerk said, "Might I ask just what you do?" I replied, "I have a continuing program of research in the laboratory and in the field. I'm working for my Masters (the whole family) and already have four credits (all daughters). Of course, the job is one of the most demanding in the humanities, and I often work fourteen hours a day. But the job is more challenging than most run-of-the-mill careers and the rewards are in satisfaction rather than just money." There was an increasing note of respect in the clerk's voice. She completed the form, stood up, and personally ushered me to the door.
>
> As I drove into our driveway buoyed by my glamorous new career, I was greeted by three of my lab assistants, ages 13, 7, and 3. And upstairs, I could hear our next experimental model (six months old) in the child development program, testing out a new vocal pattern. I felt triumphant. I had scored one on bureaucracy. And I had gone down on

the official records as someone more distinguished and indispensable to society than anyone else.

I was a mother.

The Stories Are Always Unfinished

To repeat: by its very nature, oral-aural storying resists all attempts to freeze its truth in fixed space and time. Consistency, stability, precision, and uniformity are empty categories and of no interest whatsoever to those who story (like our mother above). Such categories make no sense to them and would defeat storytelling.

On the contrary, change, emendation, plurality, expansion, revision, and the indefinite "once upon a time" form the very essence of storying. By its very nature, storying defies all those attempts at control and standardization that printed texts and modern technology have sought (successfully) to impose on the flow of nature and experience. ("It would wreak chaos on our records!")

Story seeks to define truth not through its constriction but rather its expansion. (Notice how, in our own lives, stories often expand with retelling, something we will soon note in our discussion of the biblical stories.) Story doesn't traffic in abstractions. Its truthfulness is respectfully inclusive of all the multiple meanings, alternate possibilities, and unconfined diversity of human experience. To put it simply, there are many levels to a good story, as well as different meanings at different times of one's life. You can't pin one down; truth deepens. *Pride and Prejudice* read at fifteen and at fifty-five will yield different meanings. Bible stories are very much like that: expansive, concrete, and multileveled.

Moreover, stories are often open-ended and "unfinished." We moderns have a low tolerance for unfinished business. We don't like that. We're always upset when an episode of *Law & Order* ends with a case unresolved and a fade-out shot of a puzzled assistant district attorney. We want the case tidy and finished by the end of its fifty minutes. Ambiguity unsettles us. But life *is* often ambiguous and unresolved, and storytelling allows for that. Here's an old Haggadah tale told by a rabbi:

Once there was a kingdom ruled by a very just king who

wished his subjects not only to prosper, but above all to be just and generous to one another. In this kingdom there were two farmers, landowners both, who lived one beside the other. One, the older of the two, had many sons who helped him work his land, but one left to seek his fortune in the city and another to follow a life on the sea. This left the man with a piece of good land and no one to work it. But the older farmer had other sons and more land and was still prosperous, so he decided to sell that particular piece to the younger farmer next to him. That he did, for a good and fair price. Both landowners were happy with the bargain they had struck.

But while digging a well on the piece of land he had just acquired, the second farmer found deep in the earth a coffer filled with gold coins—a buried treasure. He knew from the age of the chest and the coins that they were ancient and could not possibly have been buried by the man from whom he bought the land. Nevertheless, the second farmer went to the first and said, "Take this coffer filled with gold coins, for I found it buried on the land which I bought from you."

Now, we must stop and ask: why the second farmer would do such a thing? He had a plan. His intention was that the just king, who encouraged good works among his subjects, would hear of his generosity and hold him in special favor, probably rewarding him with greater pieces of land, or perhaps elevating him to the nobility. The seller of the land objected, however. "This treasure you have found is not mine," said he. "I did not bury it. I sold you the piece of land and got a fair price. What you found upon it is yours."

"No!" said the buyer sharply, for he was growing angry. "You must take the treasure, for I bought only the land. What was on it, or in it, is yours." "Your generosity is great, but I cannot accept," said the seller. Feeling great anger now, for his plan to win the king's favor was about to fail, the second farmer said, "You must accept the treasure I offer you, or I shall kill you."

With that, the rabbi sat back with a smile, signaling the end of his story. The people in the audience waited, and waited expectantly. "Well, get on with it, man," someone shouted, somewhat in exasperation. "What is the end of your story?" The rabbi shrugged, raising both palms upward. "Who knows?" said he. "But," insisted the interrogator, "did the buyer force the seller to take the treasure with his threat? Did the buyer kill the seller?"

"All this happened a very long time ago," replied the rabbi, "so we can be sure that the seller of the land is dead. When he died and what were the circumstances, I cannot say. All men die—though that, in itself, is no matter for mourning. For him who dies it may be a matter for rejoicing. Who can tell?"

That drives us up the wall, so conditioned are we to sound bite limits and happily-ever-after endings. But story is more true to life.

The Communal Element Lost

So, where science needs to simplify and reduce reality into clear, precise, definable categories that can be tested for their "objective truth," story comes along and questions whether such attempts at classifying human experience are ever helpful or even desirable. For the fact is, story can bear the asking of questions; story can bear ambiguity, doubt, contradiction, mystery, and enigma (again, keep in mind the biblical stories).

Story, as we just saw, can tolerate the obscure, the imprecise, the suspect, the indeterminate. Story knows that more is said through indirection, suggestion, tone, and dynamics than can ever be articulated. A print-out can't do that. Truth is in the details of teller and told. Think of the lawyer barking at the witness, "Just answer yes or no!" But you're frustrated. You can't just answer yes or no; there are shades, explanations, and nuances that must be told to get a well-rounded picture.

Again, think carefully. If coming to know the truth has ceased to be a narrative, interactive, storytelling activity, a pooling of memories and life experiences, an invoking of old traditions in new contexts, then, to put it baldly, truth no longer needs anyone else. In other words, the truth no longer needs to be arrived at by bouncing back and forth in dialogue with the collective, collaborative wisdom of a community, a region, or a people. No, it becomes "my" sole, privileged truth and my opinion is good as anyone else's. The vaunted American individualism is here. If it feels good, it's OK.

As a result, the family, clan, tribe, community of today has no common reservoir of truth, no oral traditions to hand down to one another, no stories to tell. They get it elsewhere, on an as-needed basis. And where is that? In the printed texts themselves as commodities from outside the community, centralized news conglomerates and centers of corporate power where the texts are manufactured to be consumed by the people. And, of course, if the data is delivered over TV or read in print, it must be objectively true. We live on other people's canned stories. Note the rise of the current, unqualified adoration of celebrities and the popularity of shows such as *Biography* and the reality shows. It is commonplace to observe that news has become a subdivision of entertainment.

Ah, but there's the loss: truth unmoored from context and relationship becomes a commodity: cold, impersonal, dead, absolute. Coming to know the truth is no longer a shared endeavor of mutual discussion, discernment, and participation, the interplay of minds. Instead, printed texts are slowly leaching the collective power and authority of a community and concentrating it in the hands of an elite and powerful few, who are as distanced and separated from the community as the printed words on the page are from the community's native experience. Think of the tyranny of the outside "expert" who dictates what to eat, how to dress, what's in or out; or the professor, the editor who often resembles the father in our "Flower Lady" story.

The Story Is Basic

But the fact is, story is not just a frill, an illustration, a diversion, or an entertainment, as the modern scientific mindset maintains. Instead, story is much more basic. It is a way by which and through which we come to know and understand ourselves, others, the world around us, and even God. "Have I got a story for you!" or "Let me tell you about my crazy father." In AA, therapy groups, counseling, or friendships, the invitation is always the same: "Tell me about it," because truth (and healing) will be in the person's story. Listen to one woman's assessment:

> Passing wisdom on through stories is a tradition as old as language itself. Great spiritual masters from every culture and time have relied on stories to do their teaching. Common folks have also used story as a way of passing on wisdom, and these folktales and biographical stories are equally valuable sources of inspiration and learning. Some wisdom stories are told in a simple, straightforward manner. Others speak in metaphor or are shrouded in symbolism. Some stories seek to shake us out of a logical way of thinking so that we might be opened to new understandings. Stories have many layers of meaning. We will take from them what we need and what we are ready for at the time.
>
> But why does wisdom come so often in the form of stories? The author Anthony de Mello tells of a master who always gave his teachings in parables and stories, much to the frustration of his disciples, who longed for something more to ease their understanding. To their objections the master would answer, "You have yet to understand, my dears, that the shortest distance between truth and a human being is a story."
>
> One reason that the disciples were frustrated with the stories of the master was probably that the disciples had to decipher their meanings themselves. But as one master put it, "How would you like to have someone offer you fruit and then chew it for you?" (*Doorways to the Soul,* Elisa Davy Pearmain, ed.)

That about sums up our approach to the Bible. It's a storybook that tries to pass on vision, wisdom, and a way of life. It is shrouded in symbolism and metaphors and has many layers of meaning. The only way you're going to understand it is by relating to it as an oral story, retold many times, and not as a written, once-and-for-all document.

We have to keep in mind that when we read the Bible stories in print, we are entirely outside the authors' personal, social, political, and theological storytelling context. If we don't remember that, we tend to read these stories literally and draw all sorts of weird conclusions from them. We dwell on the inconsistencies, point out the errors, and ignore the embarrassments. We focus almost exclusively on the historical facts behind the biblical texts while ignoring the authors' rhetorical practices. As children of the Enlightenment, we focus on the facts (which are "objectively" outrageous) while the biblical authors use storytelling techniques to focus on their main points. We approach the written texts with modern minds instead of entering into these original oral stories with ancient imaginations.

Taking It As It Is

Let me end this chapter by referring to David Denby. He is a film critic who, at the age of forty-eight, decided that much of the media was banal and felt he needed to take a look into the more substantive classical works of Western civilization. He studied the classics at Columbia University, and wrote a book about his experience, which was nicely titled *Great Books: My Adventures with Homer, Rousseau, Woolf, and other Indestructible Writers of the Western World*. Early on in the book he points out how different are the attitudes and values of ancient Greece from our own. Using Homer as an example, he points to unspeakable and ongoing cruelty in the *Iliad* and its unsparingly graphic descriptions of mutilation and pain and the problems these present to a different culture like ours. Denby writes:

Homer didn't have to tell his listeners that the leather

thongs, tightening as they dried, would cut into the flesh of Achilles' Trojan captives. Nor did he have to explain why Achilles later kills a Trojan warrior, an acquaintance, who begs for mercy at his knees. But how is the American reader supposed to respond to this? He comes from a society that is nominally ethical. Our legal and administrative system, our presidential utterances, our popular culture, in which TV policemen rarely fail to care for the victims of crime, are swathed in concern. Since the society is in fact often indifferent to hardship, it is no surprise that irony and cynicism barnacle the national mood.

By contrast, the Greek view was savage but offered without hypocrisy. Accepting death in battle as inevitable, the Greek and Trojan aristocrats of the *Iliad* experience the world not as pleasant or unpleasant, nor as good and evil, but as glorious or shameful. We might say that Homer offers a conception of life that is noble rather than ethical—except that such an opposition is finally misleading. For the Greeks, nobility has an ethical quality. You are not good or bad in the Christian sense. You are strong or weak; beautiful or ugly; conquering or vanquished; living or dead; favored by gods or cursed....

Academic opponents of courses in the Western classics constantly urge readers to consider "the other"—the other cultures, odd or repugnant to Western tastes, which we have allegedly trampled or rendered marginal and also the others who are excluded or trivialized within our own culture: women, people of color, anyone who is non-white, non-male, non-Western. But here, at the beginning of the written culture of the West (the *Iliad* dates from perhaps the eighth century BC), is something like "the other," the Greeks themselves, a race of noble savages stripping corpses of their armor and reciting their genealogies at one another during huge feasts or even on the field of battle. Kill, plunder, bathe, eat, offer sacrifices to the gods—what do we have to do with these ancient marauders of the eastern Mediterranean?

Denby's point is that that ancient Mediterranean culture is simply different and we should not judge them by modern, politically correct standards. We have to see it as it is. We don't have to agree, but neither should we judge from our canons. The ancient Greeks told stories in a different way with different agendas in mind. If they scandalize us, that's our problem. We have to work hard to understand what they meant, what they wanted to convey. It's the same with the older parts of the Bible, which were written about the same time as the *Iliad*. The Mediterranean biblical epic, like the Mediterranean Greek epic—both, as we said, spoken and performed long before being written down—are full of shocking cruelties, and they have to be taken on their own terms if we are to discover their message.

Denby adds these helpful words:

> My professor mentioned the contemporary resistance to reading the *Iliad*. There had been a time in the late eighties at Columbia when the yearly prospect of reading the poem in Lit Hum [humanities literature] had been greeted by dismay from some of the younger faculty. It was a poem that oppressed women and glorified war, and it had an infantile hero, and so on. I smiled to myself, because I had been thinking along the same lines, and without the benefit of any critical theory. [My professor] didn't say so in so many words, but I gathered that his opinion was that any idiot could see those things, and you could see them while never seeing what the epic poem was about. By deconstructing it or appropriating it to some modern perception of class, power, gender—none of which applies to Homer—you made the poem meaningless. The older classics, he implied, would not live if the books were turned into a mere inadequate version of the present.

And that's what people do with the Bible. Yes, it too oppresses women, glorifies war, has despicable heroes and terrible cruelty. There are some who see all that and turn it off. As a result they never see what the biblical story is all about. By projecting mod-

ern literary canons onto the oral story and current politically correct objections onto another age, they make the Bible meaningless and ridiculous.

But we would be irretrievably poorer without either Homer or
the Bible. Better, as this book attempts to do, to find a way to
come to terms with these with stories than to dismiss them
because they offend our sensibilities.

6.

UNDER THE
MEDITERRANEAN
SUN

The gap between our modern, Western mindsets and those
of the biblical Near East—the ancient Mediterranean
world— mindsets is enormous. Yet very few of us can fail
to read the ancient stories through Western eyes, and that brings a
great deal of distortion. In truth, reading the Bible is like Alice's
entering Wonderland, where all the cultural signals are subverted,
things are not what they seem and where words mean whatever
the Queen of Hearts wants them to mean: it's extremely disorien-
tating. That's the biblical world for us. Still, we insist on projecting our values and insights onto it, much to our comfort and
much to our loss. As a result, we can no longer hear what the Bible
said to its first readers who were agrarian, pre-industrial, and illiterate, and who shared a set of common cultural institutions and

patterns which persisted over a long, long period of time. They did not have our rapid change. Let's look at some contrasts.

In the biblical societies more than ninety percent of the people lived in rural areas; they farmed, fished, and took raw material out of the earth. On the other hand, ninety percent of us are urban dwellers; less than five percent of us farm, fish, or extract raw materials from the earth. Right there we have no common experiences or stories with the ancients.

Less than four percent of the ancients were literate, while in Western societies less than four percent are illiterate. The ancients had high birth rates; we have low birth rates, so much so that most European countries are now below replacement rates and it is possible that countries like Italy will phase themselves out in several generations. Life expectancy in the ancient world was about forty years, if you made it through infancy: many didn't. Ours is twice that, giving us enormous social problems with an aging population that is supported by fewer and fewer young people. Jesus, beginning his ministry at thirty was an "old" man in antiquity; he was surely older than most of his audience. Cities and villages had small populations. Jerusalem probably had at most about 35,000 people, Nazareth about 200. Contrast this to the millions and millions of people in New York and other cities.

More than half the families in the ancient world were broken by the death of one or both parents and so orphans and widows abounded. In the ancient world the whole family was the unit of production and consumption. Today in the West there is no family unit that is like that. Far from it. The Industrial Revolution has in fact been hardest on families, pulling the father out of the home and village and sending him to far-off places where the factory was located. Today, of course, with both parents working, children are subcontracted out to to day care centers while affluence scatters family members among sports, entertainment, and separate vacations. Meals eaten together as a family are virtually nonexistent; food is prepacked and prepared elsewhere, and time spent at the dinner table is measured in minutes. Family solidarity, as we shall see, was as much a given in the Mediterranean world as family segregation is in ours.

Then, too, we might mention that political life was quite unstable in the ancient world. We are shocked by the assassination of a president, but this was commonplace in the ancient world. For example, of the seventy-nine Roman emperors, thirty-one were murdered, six were driven to suicide, and four were deposed by force. Obviously, the ancient world and the modern world are far apart, and the stories more so.

With the vast gaps between the biblical world and ours, the cultural assumptions are tremendously different. That is to say, the biblical authors simply assumed their audiences knew the cultural "in" things and social clues and so took them for granted. They didn't have to spell them out or give long explanations. In other words, their written documents take much for granted just like ours do. If, for example, I refer to a "Big Mac," I rightly assume that the whole world knows what I mean and that it will instantly conjure up an image of the golden arches. I don't have to stop and explain a Big Mac, giving long descriptions and taking up a lot of print and the reader's time. I know what the reader will supply, for we are all part of the same social structures. All of us have been honed and conditioned by the mass media, exposed to the same name brands. We are all constantly under the power and influence of global corporations. Our meanings are embedded in our social system.

So it was in the ancient world. The biblical writers naturally presumed first-century Mediterranean readers and the social structures that were in place at that time, not readers of the twenty-first century post-industrial world. By way of example, when Luke tells us about Jesus' parents finding no room in the inn we immediately think of overbooked hotels or motels in crowded locations. But Luke's readers knew that Bethlehem—or anywhere else, for that matter—had no hotels or motels, and whether room was available or not depended not on who called ahead of time or got there first, but on kinship or social rank, and so Mary and Joseph were more lonely and bereft than we think.

The ancient world was one that scholars call a "high-context" society. That means that people agree on and accept and understand a broad range of shared knowledge of the context of anything they hear or read. There is simply no need of explanation. To use another example from Luke, when he writes that Elizabeth was barren, we think just that she couldn't have children, period. But the ancients knew immediately that they were reading about a terrible human disgrace and tragedy. A barren woman of that time shamed her husband, as well her own family and kin. Her social position in village life was nil, a little less than an outcast. She had no standing until she bore a son—not a daughter. All these dark overtones are lost in our society, where childless women are celebrated as liberated—think of Katharine Hepburn, Gloria Steinem, and Oprah Winfrey.

We, on the other hand, are a "low-context" society. We expect and need writers to fill us in when they write about something unusual or out of our range—and most things are out of our range. Ours is a country balkanized by specialized esoteric groups of every kind. If you're not a computer buff, for example, you don't understand megabytes and gigabytes. The old joke about dad asking four-year-old Billy how to work the computer is on target—it's another language.

Take your furnace, car, refrigerator, or central heating; take the world of plumbing, insurance, wills, engineering, sports, or music. They are all esoteric, foreign territory to most of the population. We need books for dummies to try to figure out the jargon of a particular field, or "experts" to interpret gadgets and even life for us. On Law & Order, detective Lenny Briscoe has to ask the medical examiner to "put it in English." You can't even win the lottery without immediately contacting a specialist (a lawyer). Outside of the media, which gives us an identity and a common, universal language, we are at the mercy of the experts who must explain contexts to us. Life is complicated: call Dr. Phil. The point is, we bring our low-context mentality, where we need to have everything explained, to the high-context mentality of the Bible, which needs nothing explained (all is presumed). We think the biblical writer has provided for us all we need to know when in fact most of what we need to know has not been written down. The meaning is, as we say, between the lines. And so we must somehow recover the social systems of biblical times that enable us to fill in the gaps.

Another World

I have a brother who worked for the Peace Corps. When he was sent to work in Pakistan, he first had to undergo months of inculturation in order to understand the life and history of a people who were totally foreign to him. Yet, without any background, we modern Westerners pick up the book collection of ancient Near Easterners and instantly think we know what it means.

The obvious truth, as we have pointed out, is that there is an enormous divide between our culture and the cultures—both ancient and modern—of the Mediterranean people. The social signals and assumptions are often opposed. For example, maybe when they are sad they laugh or when they are happy they weep. Maybe their villainous cowboys wear white hats and ride white horses and their noble cowboys wear black hats and ride black horses. Maybe if one of them insults me I get even with him personally, but if I insult one of them they kill my whole family. Maybe I mingle with everyone, and maybe they live in a sexually segregated society where men and women work, eat, and sleep separately. And so it goes. There are assumptions and traditions that we simply cannot relate to. These assumptions and traditions are all over their stories and writings, and we need to appreciate them. So let's look at a few differences.

Manners. We Americans are always thanking someone. Every time the waiter brings us a new dish or refills our water glass, we say thank you. We thank the taxi driver, the doorman, the store clerk, and scores of others—who should be thanking us for contributing to the economy.

In the close-knit, highly personal, intensive society of the ancient Mediterraneans, it was barter than mattered. (Money had no use in ancient culture. It functioned simply as a means of advertising: the image on the coin was the Big Boss and don't you forget it.) In this system, one would never say thank you, not because he or she was not courteous, but because it was part of the bartering system: "There is no need to thank me. You will repay me when I need something." To say thank you was to end the relationship, to indicate that you would never interact with that person again. That is why you might thank a patron, a king or nobleman who were, by definition remote and not to be encountered again—unlike your equals.

This puts the gospel story of the ten lepers into a new light. The nine didn't come back and say thanks because they were ungrateful but because they were likely to encounter Jesus again—nobody moved around much in those days—and they might need him in the future. Why terminate the relationship? On the other hand, the Samaritan's thank you indicates that he won't be needing Jesus anymore.

That close-knit, intensive society also meant that people felt free to cross each other's personal boundaries. We, who live anonymous, private lives in gated communities, cannot grasp this concept. In ancient times, men walked arm in arm. John leaned on the breast of Jesus at the Last Supper. When he healed Peter's mother-in-law, Jesus felt perfectly free to board Peter's boat without asking him. People in the same compound walked into one another's houses. The apostle Paul admonished, "Greet one another with a holy kiss" (Rom 16:16). Emotions were freely expressed, and men who did so earned honor. Ancient Romans like Caesar and Cicero openly wept, and kissed and embraced in public. Jesus readily showed distress; at Lazarus' tomb, he was "overcome by the deepest emotions" and openly wept.

Old age and youth. In the ancient world, old age was always considered better and more honorable than youth. Old persons were reservoirs of memories, wisdom, and traditions. Accordingly, respect and veneration were given to those of many years. In our modern society, the opposite is true. In their old age, people are patronized and eventually warehoused into senior villages. They are considered out of step with the new technology and the new morals. Their memories are discounted and their traditions ignored. Youth is where it's at—where the market is at.

Youth is excessively glorified in America. Television and the movies have no room for aging actors (especially women); parents are portrayed as pitiable Neanderthals, and grandparents as simpletons or comedy figures. Entire markets are devoted to youth, and they have evolved their own separate, multibillion-dollar culture. Old people are useless for production or reproduction. Their only hope is cosmetic surgery and Viagra. This excerpt from the February 18, 2004, issue of the *Wall Street Journal* tells it like it is:

> When the executive in the adjacent office returns from a two-week vacation minus any bags under his eyes or deep lines around his mouth, forget what he tells you about a certain Caribbean resort. Chances are, he has been under the knife. Cosmetic surgery, botox and other de-aging skin treatments are becoming *de rigueur* for baby-boomer executives of both sexes who fear being judged as over the hill. For many, including some top CEOs who haven't yet gone public, plastic surgery is the next step in their rigorous fitness and beauty regimens that include several hours a week at the gym, expensive personal trainers and diet consultants, and hair treatments. "I can't tell you the number of men I know who no longer are gray or who have covered bald spots with hair transplants," says Pat Cook, president of Cook Co., a Bronxville, NY, executive search firm.
>
> In addition to vanity, these executives are driven by job insecurity. They believe that looking older in business now means looking vulnerable, not wise and experienced, as might have been the case in the past. So many fifty-something managers have suffered layoffs and early retirement that survivors in this age bracket feel pressured to look and

act as young as possible to hang onto their posts. And even forty-five-year-olds who are unemployed in today's tight market worry that wrinkles will cut them out of the running.

This is surely an incredibly sad commentary on our society and its values. What a contrast to the biblical Mediterranean ideal:

Do not ignore the discourse of the aged, for they themselves learned from their parents; from them you learn how to understand and to give an answer when the need arises (Sir 8:9).

The clan and the individual. Individualism, so dear to us, did not exist in the ancient world. There were no individuals. You indelibly belonged to a clan, a tribe, a people. You were they and they were you. You were treated as part of a collective. God called the nation of Israel, not Abraham, Isaac, Jacob, or Moses for their own sakes: "You will be my people. I will be your God." The honor of the family was upheld. If a man violated another's sister not only would he be killed but his whole clan because "he" was inseparably part and parcel of that clan. This collective identity is why, in the Old Testament, words were put into the mouth of God ordering the genocide of an entire people, the Canaanites, who did nothing but were in the way of Israelite expansion (Numbers 20:14—21:3). We are properly horrified, for such a command violates our sense of justice. But from an ancient cultural point of view, it was logical. Everyone was a walking extended family, a corporate entity. We can't read our sense of fairness into another's text.

In past times, the family, both immediate and extended—and neighbors were considered extended family—was a necessary repository for identity, protection, vindication, sustenance, and survival. It was a social network central to a person's life. Any separation from the family was total tragedy as, for example, when someone with a skin disease (what the Bible calls leprosy) was forced to live outside the family and community (Leviticus 13: 45–46) and lose his life-giving network. It is no accident that when Jesus was ill-received in his hometown and the people there not only put him down (discredited his "honor," as we shall see: "Is not this the carpenter, the son of Mary...?" [Mk 6:3]) but wanted to kill him, it was Jesus' family that came to the rescue. They said, don't pay attention to Jesus, he's not quite all there. In the Middle East you could save a family member who had blundered or committed a crime if you said he was crazy.

When you left your family as Jesus did, you had to form another one. You just didn't move to an apartment in Manhattan by yourself. As we see in the gospels, Jesus joined up with Peter and his wife and clan, and along with James and John and their families, lived in Jonah's (Peter's father) communal compound in Capernaum. Luke, in his gospel, would make a big thing of a new faith family joined not by blood, but by faith and faithfulness. No matter how you slice it, family mattered.

> Jesus replied, "Who is my mother, and who are my brothers?" And pointing to his disciples, he said, "Here are my mother and my brothers! For whoever does the will of my Father in heaven is my brother and sister and mother" (Mt 12:48–50).

Marriage was a union of families, not individuals, a fusion of the honor of two families. It was always arranged (usually by the mothers) and to this extent, it was never a self-selected choice between one man and one woman. The bride and groom represented their families. Furthermore, it was a marriage between relatives (you couldn't really trust others), usually between cousins. A son would marry his uncle's daughter. Then they would live with the groom's father, along with the other married and unmarried children. Recall, for example, that Abraham would not allow his son, Isaac, to marry any of the foreign folk among whom they lived but sent him with his servant to another territory to find one of his own kin to marry, which he did (Rebecca):

> You shall not marry one of the Canaanite women. Go at once to Paddan-aram to the house of Bethuel, your mother's father; and take as wife from there one of the daughters of Laban, your mother's brother (Gen 28:1–2).

One unnerving by-product of such family and clan cohesion

was that outsiders were considered non-persons. Whenever possible you helped family and friends and friends of friends. "Suppose one of you has a friend, and you go to him at midnight and say to him, 'Friend, lend me three loaves of bread; for a friend of mine has arrived, and I have nothing to set before him'" (Lk 11:5–6). You placed your trust in group members only. Loyalty was a high virtue, betrayal the worst vice (hence the disgrace of Judas.) Those others were precisely that: "others," and there was no need to help them, aid them, or support them. Let them fend for themselves. Let them die. There was no motivation to contribute to the overall good of society. This is why, at first, Jesus ignored the Canaanite woman pleading for her daughter and said that he was sent only to the house of Israel. He was acting like a first-century Jewish male should.

If we find it hard to conceive of being so immersed in a collective clan, with well-defined, segregated roles, the peoples of old (and some modern Middle Easterners) would find it hard to comprehend our individualism. They would be amazed at modern technology that allowed a couple to pay $50,000 to an human egg donor or to find a Website where models auction these eggs off to the highest bidder. To the ancients, practices such as this and the cloning of babies would represent a radical separation from the very roots of the family, the tribe, the clan and would be an affront to the sovereign God of creation.

That couple in Bethlehem's stable, like all parents, would give their child a name that reflected the clan or its tradition or the biblical destiny of the child. Some of our parents today choose names that have no tradition, no roots, no relation to anyone in the family, but are tied into the here and now, perhaps the name of a digital celebrity or favorite product. Here are some current popular children's names gleaned from the Social Security database: Lexus, Armani, Chanel, L'Oreal, Cartier, Dior, Timberland, and Guinness. The ancients could not begin to fathom the dismemberment and segregation of families whose members don't eat together, who take separate vacations, work apart from the home, play separate sports, and have children raised by paid strangers; families in which parents and teenage children communicate on the average of fifteen minutes a day and where the youth are almost a totally separate segment of society with their own rooms, cell phones, television sets, stereo systems, recreation, and especially in this country, disposable money into the millions.

Poverty. Most of the ancients were poor and lived literally from hand to mouth. Partially because of this, they had no sense of the future; the ancient Hebrew language does not even have a future tense. They were happy to get through the day without starving and could not even think beyond tomorrow, wondering if they would survive. Planning for the future—like starting your child's college fund at his birth—was fruitless and meaningless. That's why Jesus, the Mediterranean man, told them to pray that God would give them their daily bread, enough for today, while at the same time trying to help them look ahead to God's rescue.

We cannot even begin to image the gap between the ancients and ourselves in this category. Those peasant folk could never comprehend that in the United States today, the major health problem is obesity, a condition that may soon supplant tobacco use as the number one cause of preventable deaths. Sixty-four percent of Americans are overweight; ironically, this includes the very poor who gobble up double cheeseburgers, chicken buckets, extra large pizzas, and supersized fries. The plump face of poverty would boggle the minds of the ancients, as would stores like Costco which sell such inexpensive food that it's hard not to become obese.

These forebears who, like Jesus, walked everywhere they went would be stunned not only at our cars but at their sheer numbers—230 million of them gridlocking roads, pumping pollutants into the air and, of course, eliminating the health benefits of walking. The apostles who depended on fishing for survival would be aghast at how we are sterilizing our oceans through overfishing, and how pollution has made many fish dangerous to eat. In a word, our civilization of overabundance and their civilization of need are worlds apart, and we can't appreciatively read their Scriptures, which are saturated with allusions and metaphors of dire want on the one hand and the hope of messianic abundance on the other, from our culture of excess.

Honor and shame. Honor was of extremely high value to the ancient Mediterranean peoples—as well as to those in present times. The unforgettable characters in the *Iliad* and the *Odyssey* live and die around the theme of honor. It was a core value in ancient times. Honor was the public claim to worth and the public acknowledgement of that worth. Honor was as good as it gets for the ancients and fueled all of their activity. You have to remember that, for the most part, first-century Mediterraneans lived their lives in public.

On the contrary, honor as a societal value does not rank high on our cultural list. Yes, we vaguely admire honor at a distance but it's not a top value. Some contemporary stories would puzzle the Mediterraneans: Jayson Blair, a reporter for the New York *Times*, gained notoriety for plagiarizing and fabricating news stories and was dismissed along with his editor. He had lost face (honor), as the ancients would say. But not for long in our consumer society; Blair was soon offered a six-figure advance to write a book on his shameful exploits. A dishonorable man can still make lots of money, America's certified restoration to honor.

Roman Polanski, the director, drugged and raped a thirteen-year-old girl and then fled the country before he could be sentenced. This was a most serious and shameful crime for which he, so dishonored, should have lived out his life in secret. In the ancient world he would, of course, have been killed by the girl's family to avenge her honor. But not in our culture. In 2003, the Academy Award voters honored him with an Oscar for best director. That kind of recognition would have been totally unthinkable for the Mediterranean people.

When Latrell Sprewell, a journeyman basketball player, assaulted and choked his coach several years ago, he landed a multimillion-dollar sneaker endorsement. Sports announcer

Marv Albert was caught in a messy sex scandal and was fired by NBC. But not to worry. The next year he was hired for Turner Sports and twenty-one months after his guilty plead, was rehired by NBC. Well, suffice it to say that these instances could never have occurred in the biblical world. They are cited to show the huge chasm between the ancient world and us in how we rank honor. We have to suspend our current perceptions to catch the nuances about honor that are rife throughout the Bible.

In the Mediterranean world you either inherited honor by belonging to an honorable clan or you acquired it by a noble deed. Again, to be held in honor was the highest affirmation for the Mediterranean person of any station in life. If you wanted to be somebody you had to show credentials that marked you as worthy of honor. If you were writing about your hero, you had to introduce him by first parading his right to honor. Honor was to the ancient world what celebrity is to us: a source of acceptance, fame, validation, and reputation. It was the highest good.

On the other hand, the worst possible disaster to befall someone in the Mediterranean culture was shame which, of course, shamed the entire extended clan. Shame always had to be redeemed and eradicated. In the book (and movie), *The Day of the Jackal*, the French minister who had taken up with a planted mistress told her of secret deliberations to catch the would-be deGaulle assassin, the Jackal; she in turn leaked this information to the conspirators. When he was exposed, the minister had no moral alternative. He had shamed his office and his country, and honor demanded that he commit suicide. As we saw before, in the case of a rape—a shame to the family who failed to protect the woman—honor had to be restored by killing the perpetrator and his family. To be barren in a society that extolled fertility was a terrible shame, which makes the stories of Sarah, Hannah, and Elizabeth very poignant indeed.

You can see that honor and shame are constantly at work in the gospels. Notice how the evangelists introduced their hero, Jesus. Immediately they had to establish his claim to honor because, after all, he was born to lowly people in lowly circumstances and lived in a backwater town. Therefore, the artificial genealogies in Matthew and Luke heap much honor on him: he is descended from royalty, King Abraham and King David! He is even made to be born in David's town. He is often referred to as "Son of David." Much of the friction in Matthew's gospel is due to the fact that the leaders will not accept Jesus' kingship. It is not without meaning that the sign over the cross refers to his status as king.

There are other signs of honor. The Spirit descends on Jesus at his baptism while a heavenly voice declares that he is the heavenly Father's son; you can't do better than that. Calling Jesus the son of Joseph wouldn't have gotten him very far. He gains more honor by remaining a loyal Son when tempted by the devil in the desert. In the process he shames his adversary. He gains honor as a teenager by answering the teachers well in the Temple. And people keep heaping praise on Jesus, thus affirming and increasing his honor. Luke alone offers thirty-seven examples of praise to Jesus, securing his status as a holy man. We may think this is overkill in a short book like Luke' s gospel; but Luke knew that in order for the Mediterranean people to accept the claims of Jesus, he first had to acknowledge Jesus' honor. Notice too, that since Jesus died a shameful criminal's death, his followers quickly had to turn that shame around to being an act of honor. Thus, Jesus went willingly to his death (honorably), giving his life as a ransom for many. In fact, the issue of honor was why Jesus' death was a stumbling block to the Jews and a scandal to the Gentiles.

Besides praise, honor was also maintained by clever oratory. One needed to be quick, elegant in speech, and ready for the fast sarcastic repartee. Even today there is an Arab saying that "every question is a challenge." That is, suppose you ask me something I can't answer and so shame me. So, I either ignore the question or I toss back an insult or counterquestion and so put the other on the defensive. Have you every noticed how often Jesus answers a question with a question?

Now John's disciples and the Pharisees were fasting; and people came and said to him, "Why do John's disciples and the disciples of the Pharisees fast, but your disciples do not fast?" Jesus said to them, "The wedding guests cannot fast while the bridegroom is with them, can they? As long as they have the bridegroom with them, they cannot fast." (Mk 2:18–19)

The Pharisees said to him, "Look, why are they doing what is not lawful on the sabbath?" And he said to them, "Have you never read what David did when he and his companions were hungry and in need of food?" (Mk 2:24–25)

Some Pharisees came, and to test Jesus they asked, "Is it lawful for a man to divorce his wife?" He answered them, "What did Moses command you?" (Mk 10:2–3)

Again they came to Jerusalem. As Jesus was walking in the temple, the chief priests, the scribes, and the elders came to him and said, "By what authority are you doing these things? Who gave you this authority to do them?" Jesus said to them, "I will ask you one question; answer me, and I will tell you by what authority I do these things." (Mk 11:27–29)

"Teacher...Is it lawful to pay taxes to the emperor, or not?"...knowing their hypocrisy, Jesus said to them, "Why are you putting me to the test?" (Mk 12:14–15)

They're playing the Mediterranean game of one-upsmanship. Jesus was also a master of insult. He called the Syro-Phoenician woman a dog, mocked the lawyer who asked about the greatest commandment by asking, how do you read the Scriptures; that is, you're one of the few who can read in this society and you can't understand what you're reading, you dummy? Note how often he asked his opponents, "Have you not read..." indicating that they should know better. He said in retort that his hecklers were illegitimate and had the devil for a father.

Jesus calls the Pharisees hypocrites countless times. They in turn gave as good as they got. They accused Jesus of being possessed by demons, in cahoots with the devil, and unbalanced.

These insults are not to be read as we would understand them, that is, as fast, nasty putdowns, but rather, in a Mediterranean context, as a means to establish and maintain honor and credibility in that society.

We may find all of this hard to grasp and become scandalized that the evangelists would make up fictitious genealogies and celestial signs, heavenly voices, angelic apparitions, and stories about Jesus. But again, we have to place ourselves in another time and culture. The gospel writers had to get people's attention. They already knew by faith who and what Jesus was; the resurrection was the pivotal event that had clarified this for them. With such a stunning reality that literally and figuratively put Jesus in a new light, the evangelists had to give him every credential in order to be taken seriously, so they did this according to the values and norms of their time. They were not out to deceive anyone, simply using the acceptable, time-honored literary conventions of their culture to frame the one who was Good News.

From the start, the evangelists needed to present Jesus as a holy man of great honor. Everyone one knew it was a "lie"—not a lie as an untruth, but a "lie" as a convention, just as we might address our letter "Dear John" even though John may be far from dear to us (we hate the jerk). No one takes this greeting literally. Or consider the custom of the British barristers of old in wearing wigs; this did not mean that all barristers were bald. Or when one refers to another as "my learned colleague" even though said acidly; or when everyone in the court stands to greet a suspect judge; or everyone in the halls of Congress rises to greet the President as "Hail to the Chief" is played, even though the opposition is waiting to unseat him—all these examples are conventions. Conventions are not hypocrisies. They are the necessary fictions, if you will, that a civilized society uses to remain publicly civil. Everyone understands that.

Why then should we have problems with biblical conventions? Instead of reading beyond these conventions and symbols, we have been conditioned to stop at the figures of speech themselves and so we get no further into the content. We take the scriptural words literally, applying them to our culture and not what they pointed to in the Mediterranean culture. It's like our progeny five hundred years from now reading a letter about Aunt Mary as being as sharp as a tack, or reading a reference to one's daughter as "princess," or, as I refer to my dog, "his dogship." The literalists will picture Aunt Mary's head with a pointed tip, the daughter wearing a crown, and my dog lying on velvet pillows with slaves fanning him with ostrich feathers (in this case, that actually comes close to the truth!). Remember, we are modern culture-bound Americans reading someone else's culture-bound stories, and we ought not impose our ways of thinking on them.

Segregation of the sexes. In our society where dormitories, apartments, jobs, and workplaces are freely shared between men and women, it is hard to appreciate a culture where the sexes are strictly segregated. The ancient Mediterranean society was one. Boys were considered more important than girls. Not infrequently a mother, when asked how many children she had, would reply only in terms of her sons, no matter how many daughters she had. The boys were bearers of the family honor and the avengers of family dishonor. Notice that in the Bible there are never announcements about the births of girls. Psalm 127, verses 4–5, says it all:

> Like arrows in the hand of a warrior
> are the sons of one's youth.
> Happy is the man who has his quiver full of them.
> He shall not be put to shame
> when he speaks with his enemies in the gate.

And, of course, no Mediterranean man, in a world of strict gender roles, would succumb to the modern standard of sharing the household chores. That he would cook, clean the house, and diaper the baby was unthinkable; in fact, to do so would shame and anger his wife.

Before they reached puberty, boys were raised with the women and girls; as a result, they were unbearably spoiled. They were breast fed twice as long as the girls. On reaching puberty they were unceremoniously tossed out and put into the men's camp—but momma was always emotionally reeling them back. There was no rite of passage (bar mitzvah did not exist until the fifth century AD. It goes back, like most of Judaism today, to Talmudic times.) In the men's camp they had to learn how to be a man, which meant learning how to insult (see preceding paragraphs), to grin and bear it without showing emotion. These lessons were inculcated by discipline. (Whenever you read of discipline in the Bible it always means physical punishment.) The book of Sirach, for example, gives these instructions on rearing a son:

> He who loves his son will whip him often, so that he may rejoice at the way he turns out. He who disciplines his son will profit by him…Whoever spoils his son will bind up his wounds, and will suffer heartache at every cry.…Pamper a child, and he will terrorize you; play with him, and he will grieve you.…Discipline your son and make his yoke heavy, so that you may not be offended by his shamelessness (Sir 30:1–13).

The book of Proverbs adds, "Do not withhold discipline from your children; if you beat them with a rod, they will not die. If you beat them with the rod, you will save their lives from Sheol" (23:13–14). This advice followed today would get parents into court. But, remember, physical discipline was the main way boys were taught to be men. If a father did not discipline his son, that was a sure sign that the son was illegitimate. Boys also learned how to avenge dishonor this way. The son was expected to avenge the family honor when it was besmirched, an important role in the family.

You can see all this at work in the story of Abraham and his son Isaac. The boy is obviously old enough to carry some wood on his back. When they get to the site, the lad asks where is the animal to sacrifice, and his father simply replies that God will provide. Then he takes his longed-for son, binds him, and places him on the rock, ready to slay him. We all know the story. But notice that Isaac was a true Mediterranean son. He did not scream or yell or run away when his father tied him up and placed him on the rock-altar. That would be shameful behavior. He simply said in effect, "Do what you want, dad. I can take anything you can dish out. I'm a man!" Can you image an American kid doing that? He would give his father a kick in the shin, yell that the old man's flipped, and take off while calling 911 on his cell phone.

Likewise, Jesus was a true Mediterranean man. He hung on the cross for hours without a word while others yelled, cursed, and screamed. He really could take anything they dished out. The Roman centurion cried out in admiration that this was truly a son of god. Not the Son of God in capital letters, but a son of god, one whose courage and endurance must have been given to him by the gods. Jesus "learned obedience" to his heavenly Father through suffering (Heb 5:7-10). In this context, it is no stretch at all to ask whether we can expect our heavenly Father to discipline us in the same way.

Paul was a Mediterranean man. He goes on and on about his many labors, imprisonments, beatings, shipwrecks, stoning, and so on. He was not just sounding off or being boastful. He was claiming honor. In all this physical discipline we now see abuse, but remember, that is simply our perspective. Abuse in one culture is often virtue in another. We have to resist forcing our cultural values on another culture as if we were superior.

Men and women ate separately and, outside of coming together for sex, slept separately, even husbands and wives. Men had all the power except in matters of marriage arrangements. The legend of Mary living in the Temple is just that. The Temple was a man's preserve. A woman would never be allowed inside, especially after her first period.

In our society, if faced with the choice of letting your child, wife, or mother be killed, we would all choose the child or wife to be saved. In that culture (and even today in the mid-East) the strongest bond of all is between mother and son; she would be the one chosen to be saved.

The mother, as we hinted above, controlled her eldest son. *He* was her claim to honor, not any of the daughters. Many sons meant honor multiplied. A son was his mother's protection and insurance when her husband died. Remember that when Sarah finally did have a child—and a son at that!—she ordered her stepson, Ishmael, and his mother out of the house. There were to be no rivals. Bathsheba schemed to have her husband David's other children killed so she could put her son Solomon on the throne. Mary told Jesus at Cana about failed wine knowing he would do exactly as she requested, no matter what the initial fuss.

Mothers of sons had status and took enormous pride in the achievements of their sons. ("Did I tell you about my son, the doctor?") When James and John's mother asked that her sons would sit at Jesus' right and left, she was simply acting as a normal mother. A normal mother was pushy where her sons were concerned. That daughters didn't count may offend us in our egalitarian society, but that's the way our society works, not theirs, and theirs is the one we want to understand.

Family ties, a society that values honor and scorns shame, sons who could dish out insults and keep a stiff upper lip through pain and suffering, a patriarchal system—such is the ancient world of the Bible. All the people we meet within its pages—from Abraham to Jesus—are Mediterranean people with Mediterranean values, and we have to learn to enter their world.

Part II

THE BIBLE
AS STORY

7.

RULES OF
THE STORY

A young rabbi was completely dismayed to find serious division and quarreling among members of his new congregation. You see, during the Friday evening services half of the participants would stand during one part of the proceedings while the other half would stay seated. All semblance of decency and decorum was lost as each side shouted at the other to conform to their way, with members of each group insisting that theirs was the correct tradition.

Seeking guidance, the young rabbi took a representative from each side to visit the synagogue's founder, a ninety-year-old rabbi who lived in a nursing home. "Rabbi, isn't it true that tradition was always with the people who stand at this point in the service?" inquired a man from the standing-up side.

"No, that was not the tradition," the old man replied.

"Then it is true for people to stay seated," said the sitting-down representative.

"No," the rabbi said, "that was not the tradition."

"But, Rabbi," cried the young rabbi, "what we have now is complete chaos. Half the people stand and shout, while the others sit and scream."

"Aha," said the old man, "*that* was the tradition!"

This delightful story introduces us to how oral tradition works, and it provides us with another storytelling principle. When story narratives are passed from mouth to mouth, the central point and general structure of the narrative are well preserved but the details vary according to the imagination of the current teller and the needs of the audience. Here's an example:

Joe is strong. He in fact once lifted up a car when there was an accident. This is what happened. A car was coming through the intersection of Main and Market when another car ran a light and crashed into the other car, tossing the driver, who was a man, underneath. Before the ambulance came, Joe who happened to be passing by on foot, ran over and, with a mighty heave, lifted the car up so bystanders could drag the victim clear. It was a remarkable feat. The police report of the incident was brief, objective, accurate, and precise. "Just the facts, ma'am," said the officer to a witness.

This is the attitude of the literalist, the one who is satisfied with the printed account. Whoever reads the account will not learn much. The storyteller—the way the Bible writers would tell this incident—well, that's another matter. Take a look.

Two weeks later someone is telling you the story.

"There was an accident at Main and Market. Or was it Main and Broad? Or maybe Maple Street. Or...." And at this point you're shouting, "What difference does it make! What happened?" "Well," continues the teller, "Big Joe struts over and with one hand lifts up the car like it was a bicycle and frees the woman trapped underneath."

There you are. Stories are inherently like that. This latter version, while strictly inaccurate, is not untrue. The central point and structure of the narrative are there: there was an accident and a strong man, Joe, did a remarkable feat in freeing the man underneath the car. That's intact. But what we have is an interplay of flexibility and control. The flexibility lies in the the incidental details which have been changed in the telling to enhance the point: Maple Street instead of Market, Joe is now "Big" Joe (big physically and big morally, a hero) and he doesn't run over but "struts" indicating power at work and the victim is a woman not a man, perhaps subconsciously meant to indicate a weaker sex, a more vulnerable person.

But there is control operating here as well. The control is the reality of the main event and the witnesses who were there. We might call that control "the tradition" and generally in the history of a people this tradition works at three levels. On the first level, this control is very tight when it comes to, say, poetry and proverbs. No excessive fiddling here. They're passed down as is. Otherwise, by nature, all is lost.

Then, at the next level (the biblical level, for instance), some flexibility is permitted, say, in parables and recollections of the people and the events that are essential to a people's identity. Nevertheless, the central threads, the elements in the story regarded as its core or key to its meaning, simply must be preserved and would be most fixed. The community would naturally be concerned enough to exercise strong control over its core traditions but flexibility is allowed in the details—like in the Big Joe story or the passion and death of Jesus story, where the four evangelists don't even agree on the simple sign over the cross:

Matthew: "This is Jesus, the King of the Jews"

Mark: "The King of the Jews"

Luke: "This is the King of the Jews" and

John: "Jesus of Nazareth, King of the Jews."

That's got all the elements of our "Big Joe" story: the basic event is reported, but the details are flexible. So too in Israel's memory of the Exodus. Surely the biblical numbers of Hebrews said to have left Egypt are enormously inflated (to increase the power of the deliverer, Yahweh). Thousands and thousands of people could hardly have escaped unnoticed and an event of that proportion would have been recorded in Egyptian annals and records. But the core event, enslavement, and a daring and perhaps heroic escape of even a small group, must have occurred and was read as deliverance by a God different from others.

Finally, total flexibility is allowed is such things as jokes or merely casual news. I once read a capsule review in a TV listing of *Top Hat*, the old Fred Astaire-Ginger Rogers musical. (For younger readers, Astaire and Rogers were the silver screen's most celebrated dance team, yet to be equalled much less surpassed.) The one line review read, "Silly plot, but who cares?" We catch the meaning. The plot was absurd, illogical, thin, but yes, who cares? People came to see the incomparable dance team and their romantic, dreamy dance numbers. That was the core; the plot was the detail.

We should approach the Bible in this manner. In matters essential, the core tradition will prevail as this quotation from Paul, Christianity's first canonical writer who wrote in the early 50s, insists:

> For I handed on to you as of first importance what I in turn had received: that Christ died for our sins in accordance with the scriptures, and that he was buried, and that he was raised on the third day in accordance with the scriptures, and that he appeared to Cephas, then to the twelve (1 Cor 15:3–5).

That's core tradition. The rest can be imaginative details that highlight the core.

Paul the Convert

A New Testament example will help clarify what I am saying. There are three accounts in the book of Acts of the conversion of Paul. All three are told by Luke, but all three from this very same author are strikingly different in their details. And so the critics cry, "See, it's all a fake! They can't even get the facts right!" That's the print mentality talking. But the storyteller's mentality observes the constants, such as Saul, a journey to Damascus and a mandate to persecute the followers of Jesus, a bright light, Saul's falling to the ground, his companions, and a voice from heaven. Beyond that, the details vary wildly. In one version only Saul falls to the ground, in another his companions fall as well. Only Saul hears the voice in one version but all his companions do in another. In one version Saul's blindness is underscored, in another it's not even mentioned. Ananias figures in one version and is absent in another. The commission to go to the Gentiles comes from Ananias, to Saul directly, and later at Jerusalem.

But here is the point: what tradition considered the core of the story, that is, the exchange between Saul and the exalted Christ, is told word for word in each version. Once again, the central story is held constant while the details are allowed flexibility. Moreover, as you might suspect, the flexibility underscores the main points for different audiences or different times. For example, in one version the Jewishness of Saul and Ananias is stressed to emphasize to a Jewish audience continuity with the ancient faith. In this version, for dramatic effect, the heavenly commission is delayed. We might do the same—change details and emphases—when we tell the same truth to rednecks, minorities, white collar workers, college professors, or children.

Or consider the gospels. Jesus' words had a terrific impact on people. Such words simply had to be recalled over and over again, crystallized and preserved in fixed form. They gave his disciples their identity, and when they met they must have often repeated and reflected on them. If his words were to live, the community needed to adapt Jesus' teachings for their time and circumstance. Sometimes they let go of the circumstances in which Jesus first uttered his words simply because those circumstances were now irrelevant and confusing. But they would then adapt the circumstances to fit new situations, putting words into Jesus' mouth to handle a situation he himself would not have encountered.

We see this in Jesus' (Matthew's) hostile words to the Pharisees, who were the enemies in Matthew's time, not Jesus'. Matthew is true to the spirit of Jesus' teachings, which opt for interior holiness. But he adapts and directs this teaching to a diatribe against the Pharisees who were, in Matthew's time, giving the first Jewish-Christians a hard time. In a way, all the gospels are "updated" documents for the Christians of the evangelists' times, not Jesus': their import is to ask, "How do we live as true disciples of Jesus fifty or ninety years later?" That's why they remain the repertoire of the early Church's memory of Jesus. The Jesus stories gave them guidance. Here is Scripture scholar James G.D. Dunn with a good summary of the process:

> [W]e may imagine a group of disciples meeting and requesting, for example, to hear again about the centurion of Capernaum, or about the widow and the treasury, or what it was that Jesus said about the tunic and the cloak, or about who is greater, or about the brother who sins. In response to which a senior disciple would tell again the appropriate story or teaching in whatever variant words and detail he judged appropriate for the occasion, with sufficient corporate memory ready to protest if one of the key elements was missed out or varied too much." ("Jesus in Oral Memory," in *Jesus: A Colloquium in the Holy Land*)

Hindsight

Another storytelling principle is that stories are often told in hindsight with flourish, especially those of great figures. That is, the present experience colors and elucidates the stories of the past. That's because what was in the past ran its course, so to speak, and only now is fully apparent. And so the present tends to "read back" into the past the potential that has blossomed. It's like saying, "You know, I always thought that Lincoln lad had it in him. Why I remember that when he was working in a store and accidentally overcharged a lady by a penny, he closed up and walked ten miles (it was actually five miles) to give her the penny." Now if Lincoln had not gone on to become our greatest president, this incident would have remained unnoticed. But now it's read back as an intimation of what was there all the time, a past quality that only became apparent in the light of the future.

Legends often fulfill this principle. Again, it's making Joe, our hero in the car lifting incident, "Big" Joe. The story of George Washington's refusal to tell a lie when caught with a chopped-down cherry tree might or might not be factual but it is "true" as a portent, a sign of the honesty and greatness of the man who is now one of the country's heroes and its first president. Hindsight stories elucidate and point to future qualities. And, remember, the core truth remains; the colorful details are in service to that truth.

Another principle of storytelling is that not all historical facts are literal. We see an example of this important principle in words from author Joan Windham, who wrote a delightful lives of the saints book for children. She notes:

> Most of the things I have written about really did happen to the Saints, but some of the things I have written about are just Stories that people tell about them, and these Stories are called Legends. All the Legends could have happened if God wanted it that way, and that, I think, is how most of them got started. If the Saint was a Gardening kind of a man, there are Gardening Legends about him. If he was a man who lived in a Starving place then there are Legends about plenty of Food arriving very surprisingly....And so, in this way, we find out what kind of person the Saint was, as well as what kind of things he did, by reading Legends about him.

And then she adds:

> I'll tell you something...There is a legend about me. In my garden is a pond and once I dropped a trowel into it and I nearly fell in when I was fishing it out. A very little boy thought I had fallen in and every time he sees the pond he says, "Aunt Joan fell in there!" And the other people hear him, and although it was some time ago now, a good many

people describe exactly what they think happened and how wet I was and how there were water lilies round my neck and all kinds of other stories! But they all believe that I really did fall into the pond. I didn't but it is just the sort of thing that I might have done!

So what's she saying is that even though the stories about her falling into the pond are not factual, they may well be true in the sense that they tell a great deal about her, the kind of person she is. To make an important distinction, which we shall recall again, her story is historical but not literal. Remember that. When we pick up the Scripture storybook not everything there is literal (as the fundamentalists would have you believe) but everything is historical. That is, to return to the example of our author, she really did historically exist. She did not literally fall into the pond but it's characteristic of her. Everyone who knew her would readily comment, "Whether she actually fell into the pond or not, that would be just like dear Joan, just the sort of thing she would do!"

So, we now have a capsule image of Joan, a picture of her personality type, if you will. We have an insight into the kind of person she is, what we can expect of her, and the things she would do that would be consistent with who she is. "And so in this way, we find out about the kind of a person the Saint was, as well as the kind of things he did, by reading Legends about him." It's a good storytelling insight into the Scriptures.

Overtures and Such

So while the symbolic stories of the Bible might not always be literally true, they are historically true. For example, maybe the young precocious Jesus really did confound the elders in the Temple. But maybe the story is a hindsight legend hinting at future identity, a revelatory hint of the wisdom and grace that would characterize his mission. Or take another common example which causes concern for many: the beloved birth narratives of Matthew and Luke.

Maybe, according to scholars, there were no wise men or star or choruses of angels at Jesus' birth. What we have here is the evangelists' imaginative reworking of old, recognizable scriptural symbols (called *midrash*) functioning like the overture to a Broadway musical: all the wonderful song themes are played instrumentally beforehand to give you a hint of the melodious glory to come when the curtain rises. Thus the symbols of star, magi, and angelic choruses are an overture. They are introductory fanfare—fanfare, as we shall see, with a message.

Or, to use a contemporary example, think of those loud, wild blasts of music and flashing images on the TV screen that introduce your favorite news anchor followed by the stentorian voiceover: "The 6 o'clock news with Dan Rather!" or "The O'Reilly Factor!" All that sound and fury have nothing to do with the news as such but are modern symbols announcing that a celebrity (in our society, a person of "honor"), a Notable Personage—is going to talk to you (reminding you that news, like everything else, has become entertainment). Such a technological introduction is a convention of our times.

The events surrounding Jesus' birth are just such storytelling conventions. The exotic genealogies, the star, the magi, the shepherds, and so on are conventional introductions to a significant person used in Jesus' times, just as much as a television fanfare is for a celebrity in our times. And why not? This historical person, Jesus, is a "celebrity," a Notable Personage, a man full of honor. He is important, and the celestial signs, angels, and a special star tell us so as they did for other great figures of antiquity. Moreover, Jesus' message would eventually reach out to all humankind, hence the symbolic foreigners: the magi, the non-Jews "from the East." Yes, the imaginative infancy narratives are just that: overtures to the Jesus story, historical in that they frame and point to an actual person—but not literal. They are a creative bit of storytelling for a storytelling people.

We must mention here that for Christians, the real curtain-riser after the overture was the experience of the Risen Jesus. That mega-event colored everything else and was consistently read back into the four gospels, helping to provoke the story symbols that shaped the gospels. As Thomas Rausch writes in his excellent book, *Who Is Jesus?*:

> The Gospels and other New Testament documents are written in the light of the Resurrection and of the disciple's Easter experience of new life in Jesus; they are products of Christian faith. Though there is considerable historical memory enshrined in the texts...they do not count as historical writings in the modern sense. They were written to proclaim faith in the risen Jesus present in the Christian community and in the lives of the disciples, not to document the story of his life as a modern historian might do.

As a slight interruption, it might be worthwhile here to insert just what that "historical memory" or core tradition about Jesus is when all the storytelling hindsights and flourishes of the gospels are removed. A good summary can be found in a summary given by Rausch, which he gleaned from Luke Timothy Johnson's book, *The Real Jesus*:

> Jesus was a human person and a Jew (Paul, Hebrews, NCW [Non-Christian Writings]), of the tribe of Judah (Hebrews) and a descendant of David (Paul). His mission was to the Jews (Paul, NCW); he was a teacher (Paul, James, NCW), was tested (Hebrews) and prayed using the word Abba (Paul). He prayed for deliverance from death (Hebrews), suffered (Paul, Hebrews, 1 Peter) and interpreted his last meal with reference to his death (Paul and by implication, Tacitus and Josephus). He underwent a trial and appeared before Pontius Pilate (Paul, NCW); his end involved some Jews (Paul, NCW). He was crucified (Paul, Hebrews, 1 Peter, NCW) and was buried (Paul). After his death, he appeared to witnesses. (Paul).

The gospel narratives play on those core memories highlighting them with the patina of the resurrection. That's the verifiable core synthesis of the life, death, and resurrection of Jesus, the scholar's outline. Still, for us, that outline, even when fleshed out in the gospel accounts and expanded by pious writers, remains ho-hum. Familiarity with the Jesus story has bred the contempt of resistance. That's why it's worthwhile, I think, to read a modern secular Jew's encounter with the Jesus of the New Testament. Here's David Denby:

> The man whose likeness glowed on calendars and posters in nacreous pallor, as if lit from within by dim fluorescent light; the Redeemer whose plastic body swung from taxi-drivers' dashboards and whose gaze, a column of light in old Hollywood movies, loosened the bowels of Victor Mature and struck Charlton Heston dumb, this Jesus, when encountered in his original form, was an amazing figure who laid down one challenge after another. Reading again, I was forced to put away the kitsch of Christianity, forced to touch its core, and I was stirred.
>
> "If thine eye offend thee, pluck it out," Jesus said. No matter how metaphorically one reads that extraordinary sentence, it becomes no less exciting. You were just to leave, accept the call to follow Him and leave, walking out on your house, your wife and children, your mother and father. To reach God, you had to reject an intolerable patch of your soul. And this was no soothing and consoling message of charity and acceptance; it was as radical a demand as had ever been offered to people who thought they understood what virtue was. Even turning the other cheek to be struck, which many now consider bizarre, a weak, even masochistic act…even this could be seen as a kind of triumphant thwarting of the enemy. You undermined his hostility, sending it back as love. You astounded him by giving him more than he wanted, the cloak as well as the coat, and you shamed his greed.
>
> Someone will rightly object that I am ignoring for my own convenience the spiritual and emotional power of the Gospels—the reality of Jesus' death and resurrection, the immeasurable sacrifice he made for man, the narrative of a

man scourged, mocked, and crucified. Maybe so, but when someone who is not a Christian reads the Passion story, what strikes him most strongly is Jesus' extraordinary presence of mind, his strength and shrewdness as well as sweetness, and his toughness, which at times is stunning—a spiritual power that derives, in part, from intellectual high spirits and good health. Incomparable intellectual vitality overcome by the necessity of death—that was my non-Christian view of Jesus.

So, even as we ponder these words, what do we conclude from this chapter? We can conclude that the oral-aural tradition goes back to the time of Jesus. We do not always have an account of his exact deeds and words—we must acknowledge that. What we *do* have is the impact they made that goes back to his actual words and deeds.

The effect of the Easter theophany, its translation from Aramaic to Greek, and the transition from a little Galilean village like Capernaum to a Hellenistic city like Corinth highly affected and shaped the Jesus tradition which was adapted to current local tensions and conflicts. So it is that in the gospels, for example, you have both history (reinterpreted) and theology. How could it be otherwise? But, all the more, the oral Jesus tradition provided the essential living link to him. This is precisely why that tradition was cherished and fixed in writing as well as in the liturgy.

8.

THE ORAL TRADITION

L et me add another principle of storytelling. If the reliability of the oral tradition controls the core story, the storyteller's intent, needs, and audience control the details. That's the way storytelling works. So, for example, in the story of Big Joe, when told in a place where there are no cars and the people have never even heard or seen one, the teller might say that the man was run over by a horse and wagon. The core story and its dynamics are the same but the story doesn't have to be interrupted for explanations. Or, in our modern society, if we really want to emphasize the incident we could say, "And this humongous Hummer barreled through the stop sign and creamed the man."

In either case, do we really want to fuss and correct the storyteller? The point is there. Or, if the tale of the Good Samaritan is told in a place where apartheid reigns, the teller might make a substitution:

Now by chance a priest was going down that road and when he saw him, he passed by on the other side. So likewise a Levite, when he came to the place and saw him, passed by on the other side. But a black man while traveling came near him; and when he saw him, he was moved with pity. He went to him and bandaged his wounds... (Lk 10:31–34).

The core tradition in this story—that Jesus resonated with the poor and powerless, ate with sinners and those outside the law, embraced little children, and had pity on the crippled and blind—is beyond doubt. It is perfectly consistent with that tradition, therefore, to tell a Jesus story with a change of detail that makes Jesus' message and mission relevant to those who most need them. Yes, the rational skeptic might complain, "Come on, it was either a white Samaritan or a black American. Check the record. Another instance of error in the Bible!" But that's the print mentality at work, not the imagination unleashing the power of story and the revelation of a God of pity and love.

Another principle is that story is "soft." It is human. It allows for and even seems to rejoice in contradiction. How about this:

Mom is in the kitchen when she hears son Billy retreating hastily into the house shouting to his playmate, "You liar! You liar!" He runs into the kitchen where mom tries to calm him down as, quite upset, he tells her about Bobby, his friend, saying nasty untruths about his father. After mom soothes him with milk, cookies and a hug, she tells Billy never to call anyone a liar. "That's a harsh term. It's not nice no matter what they say to you. Prove yourself bigger."

About two weeks later, Billy comes home and he hears his mother on the phone saying, "Oh, Jane, that's terrible! It's simply not true. She's a liar." No sooner are the words out of her mouth than she turns and sees Billy standing there open mouthed. Dum-da-dum dum. "Jane, I'll call you back." She bends down and says, "Billy, I was wrong. I shouldn't have said that especially when I told you not to use the word. I was excited and upset and I'm sorry. It's not a nice word and

I shouldn't have said it and won't say it again. And neither should you. O.K? Now, go change your clothes."

This is a very human situation and everyone has a sense (except the hard-nosed critics) that the mother was not being hypocritical. The teaching still held. The guidance still remained valid. Her slip of the tongue didn't undo or contradict anything. It was just one of those things that people do and everyone instinctively understands. And maybe it's also an object lesson to Billy that everyone make mistakes and it's all right.

Anyway, with this story in mind, we turn to Matthew 5:22. Jesus is calmly teaching: "Whoever says, 'you fool!' shall be liable to the hell of fire…." Later, in the very same gospel, Jesus is annoyed with the Pharisees and he spits out (like a true Mediterranean man), "You blind fools!" (23:17). Uh-oh. Those with too many initials after their names cry fraud, contradiction, unreliability. But most folks take it as it is: a very human situation that doesn't undo any teaching or make the story of Jesus any less valid or truthful. The evangelist is telling a story and he includes all the human elements in it. People lose their cool not their principles, and Jesus is no exception. He who grew weary sometimes and overthrew Temple tables and wept and suffered and died as we do fits into our human story. Which is why, once more, it is best to view Scripture as a story and not as a legal brief.

I might add that story is easygoing and pokes fun at itself. To wit:

The great rabbi was dying and, as we all know, deathbed wisdom is the best. So his students lined up, single file, to receive his last words. The most brilliant student was at bedside, the second most brilliant student behind him, and so on, till the line ended at a pleasant enough fellow who was a good room and a half away. The most brilliant student leaned over to the slowly slipping rabbi and asked, "Rabbi, what is the meaning of life?" The rabbi groaned, "Life is like a cup of tea." The most brilliant student turned to the second most brilliant student. "The rabbi said, 'Life is like a cup of tea!'" And the word was whispered from student to student till it arrived at the pleasant enough fellow who was biting his nails a room and a half away. "What does the rabbi mean, 'Life is like a cup of tea'?" he asked. And the word was passed back up the line till the most brilliant student leaned once again over the slowly slipping rabbi. "Rabbi, what do you mean, 'Life is like a cup of tea'?" The rabbi shrugged, "All right, then, so maybe life is not like a cup of tea!"

We enjoy these stories. Yet, in a sense, we're disturbed in a way we can't explain. God's word, God's revelation should be more formal, more precise, more, shall we say, doctrinal so we know where we stand. There should be no margin for error or misunderstanding. Everything should be neat and exact; anything less is suspect. But that's our print, Enlightenment, "scientific" minds talking. Life just isn't like that and because it isn't, we need our truth wrapped in story so that we can allow some flexibility, some challenge, some teasing and, yes, some imprecision.

To put all this formally, we can turn to the Instruction of the Pontifical Commission called, *On the Historical Truth of the Gospels*, issued in 1964, which says that the gospels developed in three stages. First there was the oral stage, which is the time of Jesus and his apostles, during which he taught and acted, died and rose. This would be between 30 and 33 AD. The second stage is the preaching stage after Jesus had died and risen, when his followers preached Jesus and all that he did and taught. We're talking about the years 33 to 53 AD.

The third stage, says the Commission, is the stage where the Gospels were written down by second generation, non-eyewitnesses, which included collecting the Palestine stories about Jesus, editing and adapting them to another (Greek) culture, and upgrading the message for the writers' time, place, and needs of the community. The time frame during which all of the canonical New Testament books were written down would be about 53 to 90 or 95 AD. Of course, people continued to fiddle with them, correcting, adding, and subtracting a bit here and there well into the third century. This means that the writers retained the sense of the sayings of Jesus but did not express them word for word as he said them in his time and place. They put words in Jesus' mouth that were appropriate for their time and place. After all, the writers were not interested in reporting the words of Jesus so that they could be memorized but that they might become a basis for faith.

Editors at Large

Let's continue. There's no doubt that Matthew and Luke edited the text of Mark, the first and earliest gospel: abbreviating; adding material to make or further a point, or sometimes to clarify an issue or avoid misunderstandings; adding insights that could only come with time (such as the impact of Easter and its meaning for the Christian community). Here's a simple case: think of Luke changing the roof construction of Mark from thatches to tiles in the story of the paralyzed man whose friends lowered him through the roof in front of Jesus. Mark's more early and more Jewish audience knew about thatches on roofs, but Luke's sophisticated Greek audience wouldn't know a thatch if they fell over one. So Luke changed the roof material to tiles, which the Greeks were familiar with. He wisely changed a detail but kept the core story intact. Matthew and Luke corrected Mark on some geographical points. (Apparently Mark flunked geography in school.) In some of his writings he has described locations in a way that would be similar to placing Rhode Island next to Delaware. What did he know? He wasn't in Palestine. He had the core stories, but not the details.

It's worth a detour here to make a careful observation: if we think that all of Matthew's and Luke's reworkings are solely the literary task of tidying up Mark's writing (or copying from "Q," a theoretical collection of the sayings of Jesus), we would be mistaken. After all, remember that Matthew and Luke also heard the oral stories many times about Jesus—how could they not?—and they could easily be using their oral version of the same story found in Mark. This may have occurred more often than we think, and so Matthew's and Luke's retellings could well result more from oral sources than from copying the written words of Mark. If you will, Matthew and Luke had the "Maple Street-Big Joe" oral version of the story; Mark had the first "Market Street-Simple Joe" oral version. In both cases, the core is essentially the same. The tradition, as we said, would see to that.

The details can vary and that explains, as much as anything else, the different twists and even some errors ("Maple Street")— but it doesn't change anything. As James G.D. Dunn puts it so well,

> These are all teachings remembered as teachings of Jesus in the way that oral tradition preserves such teaching, with the character and emphasis of the saying retained through stable words and phrases, but the point elaborated in ways the re-teller judged appropriate to the occasion. ("Jesus in Oral Memory")

Don't we do the same when we tell a story?

Another good example is the Sermon on the Mount. Neither Matthew or Luke were eyewitnesses to this event. They depended on the oral stories for their accounts. Most likely the sayings of the Sermon on the Mount were given at various times, then collated into a kind of "mission statement" about Jesus. The sayings contain the core teaching of Jesus, but the two evangelists change the details for a reason. Matthew has Jesus delivering these sayings on a mountaintop while Luke has Jesus delivering them down on the plain. For fundamentalists, who read the Bible literally, the only out is to say that Jesus, like all good teachers, gave his lesson twice, once on the mountain and another time in the valley. For those who know the rules of storytelling, this is not necessary.

Matthew, writing for a Jewish audience, knew how important it was to tap into the Jewish devotion to Moses and his laws. So, in true storytelling style, he kept the core tradition and added the critical detail that Jesus gave the new commandments, from the mountain because that's where Moses received the commandments. The unmistakable message is that Jesus is indeed another Moses. He stands in the great Old Testament tradition. He is not an innovator but a fulfillment: "Folks, we have another Moses here before us. Listen to him." But Luke—well, he is the writer of sensitivity and social concerns. After all, we have Luke to thank for the parables of the Prodigal Son and the Good Samaritan, as well as Jesus' connection to the common people. He could never have Jesus preach from a grand mountaintop pulpit. He would have to be down on the plain mingling with the poor, the unwashed, the unwanted, and those outside the law.

The core tradition of Jesus' teaching, mercy, and compassion remains in both these accounts, but the storytellers highlight the tradition in the way they deem most effective. Flexibility is at work with tradition. And so, when you hear the familiar mantra, "A reading of the holy gospel according to Matthew (Mark, Luke, or John)," you should think, "Ah, we're hearing Matthew's telling of the Jesus story and we had better turn our minds to his audience and to the way he frames his story. Let's climb the mountain and sit at the feet of the new Moses." For Luke, it's down into the alley-ways with a male Mother Teresa. For Mark it's running to keep up with the divine Mad Hatter, and with John it's a kind of New Age guru not quite of this world speaking beautiful thoughts.

And the core tradition, in spite of flexibility and all the "according to's," is really there because of what Aramaic scholars have long pointed out; namely, that the Aramaic oral tradition behind the Greek translations of the gospels is clearly evident in stylistic features such the parallelisms, rhythms, assonances, and alliterations that are so characteristic of spoken Aramaic. In other words, many of the Jesus sayings in the Greek gospels clearly betray Aramaic origins and that, in turn, once more shows the persistence and accuracy of the oral narrative.

And, as Lieutenant Columbo would say, "one more thing": even when the evangelists *did* write down the tradition they knew and their works were passed around, remember that the congregations who received them were not receiving new revelations.

They already possessed in their corporate memory their own oral or written versions of much of the evangelists' material about Jesus, and they would make comparisons between the accounts. In some cases, it's possible that a congregation would prefer their version of a story over Luke's or Matthew's.

The Liturgy

Here I must also point out another way the oral narrative endured: through the liturgy. Liturgy by nature is quite conservative, and it preserves old traditions and stories by repetition. A case in point would be the Our Father, which we still communally recite at Mass. If you compare Matthew's version with Luke's, they are somewhat different. Matthew gives us a the "full version" of the Our Father and Luke gives us this:

> Jesus said to them, "When you pray, say: Father, hallowed be your name. Your kingdom come. Give us each day our daily bread. And forgive us our sins, for we ourselves forgive everyone indebted to us. And do not bring us to the time of trial" (Lk 11:2–4).

What you have here is not just a shorter version of the same prayer, but another instance of storytelling where the core is the same and the details differ. People in different places simply had different oral versions of the same episode, and both versions became part of the early Christian liturgical worship. It's as simple as that. The early Christians knew their prayer version because they prayed it daily and the differing versions simply show diverging patterns of liturgical adaptation. So Matthew's church prayed one way and Luke's another. There is no contradiction, no need for effort at trying to reconcile the two prayer forms. They're the same prayer. They merely reflect an oral telling: the core is the same, the liturgical details differ.

The same could be said for the words of the institution of the Eucharist at the Last Supper. The differences in Matthew, Mark, and Luke reflect liturgical differences. The three evangelists recorded these variants not because they were reading each other's scripts and improving one another's words, but because these were the words they heard when, as we would put it, they went to church. The words were a living oral tradition before they were ever set down. Paul, the first Christian writer in the Bible, also was very careful to pass on accurately the tradition begun by Jesus and he too places that tradition within the liturgy. Scripture scholar John Meier says it well (italics mine):

> [Jesus'] words at the Last Supper were probably a simpler form [than any of the gospel versions], one that has been expanded in different ways by the liturgies of the early church and by the New Testament writers. Like the variant forms of the Lord's Prayer and the Beatitudes, the variant forms of the eucharistic words remind us that *the early church was interested in preserving the substance, the essence, the core message of what Jesus said, not the exact wording.* In that, the evangelists operated like many an historian in the ancient world: nobody told the evangelists that they had to operate like twentieth-century historians instead.

So storytelling and an oral core are behind the Scriptures. And, naturally, so are storytellers. They combine to create fresh interpretations for their listeners (readers).

A brief, final principal of storytelling is that stories assume. That is to say, as we have already hinted, that the teller assumes his audience can fill in the gaps. If I say, "As Oprah said," I don't have to pause to explain who Oprah is. I don't even have to use her last name; I assume you know it. If I say that President Bush (at this writing) spoke of an assassination in Egypt, I assume that one of his aides told him about it. He wasn't there. So in the gospel of Mark, Pilate asked Jesus, "Are you the King of the Jews.?" This Jesus is only one of many prisoners brought before him. How did Pilate know enough about Jesus to bring up this subject? The story assumes that someone prepped Pilate. If in Matthew (27:2) the chief priests have already taken off to hustle Jesus away to Pilate, how can they still have been in the Temple one verse later when Judas returned with the thirty pieces of silver? You have to assume that all this was happening at the same time and picture the scene in your mind.

A story from India, "The Three Dolls," provides a good closing summary to all we have written thus far:

There was once a king who considered himself a great and clever king. He would proudly stroke his long beard and proclaim: "Ah! I am a clever king! To demonstrate my cleverness, I invite anyone to challenge me with a riddle or puzzle to solve." One day, this king received a package containing three dolls, and a challenge which read: "Oh, King, if you are as great and clever as you maintain, please be so wise as to tell the difference between these three dolls." The king announced: "Aha! I am a great king and a clever king, and I shall easily solve this little riddle."

So the king stroked upon his beard and hummed to himself as he studied the three dolls: "Hum-hum-hum, hum-hum-hum, hum hum-agh!" He pulled upon his beard in frustration, for he could see no difference between the dolls. The three dolls were exactly alike, in every form and feature, down to the minutest detail. "Aha!" thought the king. "I am a great king and a clever king. And it is said that a great king will keep a wise man nearby to help him solve his problems. I have such a wise man." Then he called for the wise man. The wizened old wise man hobbled into the court. Leaning upon his staff, he bowed before the king. "Majesty. In what wise matter may I be of service?" "Wise Man," said the king, "I have before me three dolls, exactly alike. What is the difference between them?" The wise man bent to examine the dolls. After a great deal of consideration, the wise man thought to tell the king this matter was not worth his time. He thought to tell the king many other things, too, but finally he wisely said nothing. For it is wise to keep your thoughts to yourself, especially in the presence of a powerful monarch. The king sent the wise man away.

"This wise man is of no use to me," thought the king. "He is too shrewd. But I am a great king and a clever king, and it is said that a great king will sometimes listen to the council of a fool. For a fool will rush in where wise men fear to tread. I have such a fool." Then he called for the fool. The fool indeed rushed in, slapped the king merrily upon the back and said, "Hi ya, King! How 'ya doin'?" "Fool," said the king, "I have three dolls exactly alike. What is the difference between them?" The fool did not listen. He saw the three dolls and only thought to play with them. "Whee! Dollies! Let's play pretend! Let's pretend we're going on a picnic!"

But before the fool could have much fun, the king sent him away. "This fool is of no use to me," thought the king, "for this fool is a fool! But, I am a great king and a clever king, and it is said that a great king will retain a storyteller. For the tellers of tales carry in their stories many words of wisdom." He called for the storyteller. Into the court came the storyteller, bowing low with a great flourish. The storyteller began to speak at once. "Majesty, how may I serve you? A fable, perhaps? Or a recitation of the glorious deeds of your greatness in verse and song? Or perhaps...."

"Enough," commanded the king. "Storyteller, don't get started. Today I have a riddle " "Ah! Such as the riddle of the Sphinx?" the storyteller interjected. "Or the riddle of the little man who spun straw." "Precisely!" The king held up his hand to keep the storyteller from speaking further. "Now listen: I have three dolls exactly alike. You are a teller, can you tell the difference between them?" The storyteller studied the three dolls briefly and exclaimed, "Majesty, you cannot see any difference between these dolls!" "That much myself I have already determined," groaned the king. "Majesty," said the storyteller, "if you cannot see a difference between these dolls, the answer must be much like the story of the three caskets: their outward show is greatly different from that which they contain. Likewise, the differences between these three dolls must be within." "Ah, very good," said the king. "But how can you show these differences?"

"Majesty, there must be many ways to reach inside a person. However, the one way with which I am most acquainted is through the ears. If you will permit me." The storyteller reached up and plucked a hair from the king's beard. "Ow!" exclaimed the king. "How dare you?" "Forgive me," begged the storyteller. "But as you shall see, it was most necessary." He then lifted the first of the three dolls and began to thread the king's hair into the doll's ear. The hair went in and in and in the doll's ear until it was gone. "Majesty," said the storyteller, "this doll must be a wise man. What it hears, it keeps to itself!" "Very good," said the king. "And what of these others?" "If you will permit me," said the storyteller, and again he plucked a hair from the king's beard.

"Ow!" winced the king. Now the storyteller lifted the second doll and began to thread the hair into its ear. The hair went in and in and in. But as he was threading the hair in one ear, it came out the other. "Majesty, this doll is obviously a fool: what goes in one ear comes out the other. " "Very good," said the king. "And this last one?" "If you will permit me." "Ow!" Once more the storyteller plucked a hair. Lifting the third doll, he began to thread the hair into its ear. The hair went in and in and in. It did not come out the other side, but it did not stay altogether in, either. For as he was threading the hair into the doll's ear, it came slowly out the doll's mouth. "Majesty, this doll is a storyteller: what it hears, eventually it tells."

The king looked at the three dolls. "Storyteller, you have solved this riddle. But I see you have given me a new riddle to consider. For when you put the hair in the doll's ear, it is a straight hair. Yet, when the hair comes out the doll's mouth, it is all curled. Why?" "Majesty," said the teller, "no storyteller worth his salt will ever tell a tale exactly as he heard it. We must always add a special curl of our own devising in the retelling of the tale!" And so have I done in retelling this tale for you. (*Ready to Tell Tales*, ed, David Holt and Bill Mooney).

If you will see the evangelists as storytellers who never tell the Jesus tale exactly as they heard it but add a special curl of their own devising, you won't stumble over the differences or contradictions or incorrect details. Instead, you won't merely read the frozen text, but in imagination you will listen to the core oral tradition behind their words and what they are trying to convey about that incredible man from Nazareth.

9.

BIBLICAL CURLS

L
et's move in a wider circle. Memorization, a strong component of the ancient mind—incredible compared to our
dependence on papers and computers—and honed by constant repetition, guaranteed that the core story remained firm.

In rabbinic Judaism, the pupil had the solemn duty to maintain his master's exact words. So it was with Jesus' disciples. They
hung on every word, repeated them often, memorized them, gave
them great authority, had mnemonic devices to remember them,
and even retold them during Jesus' lifetime. Thus, by the time
these stories were written down, the central point and main structures were intact—even if the details were changed and at times
erroneous. Mark's gospel, for example, shows all the signs of an
text copied from oral traditions, a "written orality" we might say.
And, we must remember, that even when the words and deeds of
Jesus were written down, they were written in an age of great illiteracy; therefore, the texts themselves were very much meant to be
heard like a performance (and I wouldn't be surprised if the reader didn't add a frill or two in the exercise).

So, there are three things we might remember. First, all this gives us a better handle on the "errors" of the Bible. The Bible is replete with factual errors, duplications, and revisions. But, to put it simply, they are mostly of the Market Street-Maple Street variety. That is, the details have been lost or forgotten or were skewed to fit differing audiences. They are wildly flexible even to the use of another nation's myths (which grates on our modern "just-the-facts, ma'am" mentality) and freewheeling (which offends our print mentality), but the core story, critical and important to self-identity, is regulated and warrantied, as it were, by tradition. That's why, when we read the Bible, we must resist the literary mindset that distinctly asks, "What does it say?" and move to the storyteller mindset that instinctively asks, "When the story is said and done with, what does it all mean?" And if someone declares, "This is the one and only meaning," toss the bum out.

Second, I repeat: we must learn to jettison our literacy-print lens when we pick up the Bible. Try to remember that you are picking up an anthology of stories from different eras, written in different styles. The Bible is not a collection of scientific papers. It's a collection of oral stories. Try to hear the voice behind them. Don't get hung up on the "mistakes," verbal gaffes, and contradictions. Try to pick out the core tradition.

Take dear old Santa Claus, for example. He has mightily metamorphosed throughout the centuries, starting as the very real St. Nicholas of Myra, a small, simple, lean, bishop with a big heart. In the storytelling journey we find that Santa can be tall or short, smooth-faced or bearded, clothed in bright purple, forest green, or the red suit created by cartoonist Thomas Nast. He can be as rotund as Pavarotti or as slim as Barney Fife. He can drop a sack of money through an open window (an act attributed to Nicholas of Myra) or he can climb down chimneys with a sack of toys. He can travel by foot (as bishop Nicholas did) or fly through the air with eight reindeer, led most recently by one with a shiny nose. In short, Santa (meaning "holy" or "saint") can do many different things and don many different outfits, but there's one thing Santa can never be: a child abuser. After all, he derives from St. Nicholas (the core story) who in turn derives from the Christ Child, who derives from the Father of all gifts.

Compassion and generosity are forever locked into the core tradition of Santa Claus. The core tradition would not, could not, permit a connection between Santa and violence when the whole point of the character is benevolence and kindness (except, of course, in the hands of nihilistic filmmakers). Details can and do vary according to culture, changing times, and the imagination of the storyteller, but still the tradition protects the image from intrinsic contradiction. That is why, even as we shamelessly commercialize Santa, he must still retain his core origins: one who, in the name of Jesus, was compassionate and generous to "these little ones." No one really frets over the details (is he thin or is he fat?). We get the point. So it is with the biblical stories.

Or take something that people are apt to hear these days, especially from preachers who suffer from too much learning: there were no Magi! Further, the whole infancy narrative is one big fiction! The answer to this, as we noted two chapters earlier, is yes, it is. The print mentality regards this fact dismissively. But as we have seen, the storytelling mind sees differently and would rather say that, yes, the magi story is not literal but it is historical.

This story, in fact, dips into the Old Testament story of Balaam in the Book of Numbers (chapter 22) whereby a seer from the East (Balaam) was asked by the King of Moab to come and curse his enemy, Israel. But Balaam, much to the chagrin of the King of Moab, winds up blessing Israel (and, of course, gets fired):

> God who brings him out of Egypt, is like the horns of a wild ox for him; he shall devour the nations that are his foes and break their bones. He shall strike with his arrows. He crouched, he lay down like a lion, and like a lioness; who will rouse him up? Blessed is everyone who blesses you, and cursed is everyone who curses you (Num 24:8–9).

By the way, inserted in this Balaam episode is the somewhat humorous story of his talking donkey, an instance of pure, classic folklore. In any case, the point is that a man from the East brings God's revelation about Israel. And Matthew, a good story-teller, models his magi after them. (His audience would have known the Balaam story). They are gentile non-Israelites from the East, using what natural means they have (the reading of the stars) to find and adore God—although they needed the Jewish Scriptures to find out precisely where this infant God is ("And you, Bethlehem...from you shall come a ruler who is to shepherd my people Israel" (Mt 2:6).

The magi, in short, are Balaam. They are his story counterpart. These gentiles come from the East to bring revelation about this Child and to bless Israel (by offering gold, frankincense, and myrrh). The magi story is a way of conveying the truth that salvation is open to all and can be found by all. Concerning this whole Christmas episode of magi, stars, angels, and shepherds—in fact, as a summary of the whole concept of truth wrapped in story—carefully read these words of that wonderful author, Frederick Buechner:

> We live in a skeptical age where the assumption that most of us go by, consciously or otherwise, is that nothing is entire-ly real that cannot somehow be verified by science. It seems to me at best a dubious assumption, but it is part of the air that we breathe, so let us be as skeptical as our age about this story of Christmas. Let us assume that if we had been there that night when he was born we would have seen nothing untoward at all. Let us assume that the darkness would have looked very much like any darkness. Maybe there were a few stars, the same old stars, or the moon. For a long time the only sound perhaps was the rough, rapid breathing of the woman in labor. If the tradition of the manger is accurate, there was the smell of hay, the great moist eyes of the cattle. The father was there, possibly a shepherd or two attracted by the light, if there was any light. There was a last cry of pain from the mother as the child was born, and then the cry of the child. In the distance maybe the lonely barking of a dog.

The mother stares up at the rafters from where she is lying, too exhausted even to think of the child. Someone has taken him from her to wrap him up against the cold and darkness of the world. Maybe a mouse burrows deeper into the straw.

Maybe that is all we would have seen if we had been there because maybe that or something like that was all that really happened. In the letters of Paul, which are the earliest New Testament writings, there is no suggestion that the birth of Jesus was accompanied by any miracle, and in the gospel of Mark, which is probably the earliest of the four, the birth plays no part. So a great many biblical scholars would agree with the skeptics that the great nativity stories of Luke and Matthew are simply the legendary accretions, the poetry, of a later generation, and that were we to have been present, we would have seen a birth no more or less marvelous than any other birth. But if that is the case, what do we do with the legends of the wise men and the star, the shepherds and the angels and the great hymn of joy that the angels sang? Do we dismiss them as fairy tales, the subject for pageants to sentimentalize over once a year come Christmas, the lovely dream that never came true? Only if we are fools do we do that, although there are many in our age who have done it and there are moments of darkness when each one of us is tempted to do it. A lovely dream. That is all.

Who knows what the facts of Jesus' birth actually were? As for myself, the longer I live, the more inclined I am to believe in miracle, the more I suspect that if we had been there at the birth, we might well have seen and heard things that would be hard to reconcile with modern science. But of course that is not the point, because the Gospel writers are not really interested primarily in the facts of the birth but in the significance, the meaning for them of that birth just as the people who love us are not really interested primarily in the facts of our births but in what it meant to them when we were born and how for them the world was never the same again, how their whole lives were charged with new significance.

Whether there were ten million angels there or just the woman herself and her husband, when that child was born the whole course of history was changed....This is what Matthew and Luke were trying to say in the stories about how he was born, and this is the truth that no language seemed too miraculous to them to convey. This is the only truth that matters, and the wise men, the shepherds, the star are important only as ways of pointing to this truth. (*The Hungering Dark*)

Savor that. It's Bible as story in a nutshell.

The Apocryphal Gospels

Let's move on to something that seems to fascinate the public: the apocryphal gospels, those that didn't make it into the official canon of four gospels. A sensationalist press eagerly pounces on these gospels, darkly suggesting that they were suppressed by the Church because what really happened was that Jesus didn't die at all but came down from the cross, married Mary Magdalene, and ran off to India!

The best selling book by Dan Brown, *The Da Vinci Code*, high on suspense and low on facts, plays on the old, hoary, conspiracy theories. Although it teems with historical misinformation, I must mention that, at this writing, it is still popular and has generated tons of press and media attention. Why not? Lies, sex, intrigue, suppression: it's all there, all the standard media assessments of the evil Catholic Church. As I write this, the book is being made into a movie directed by Ron Howard. Once more the theme will play out that the Catholic Church had systematically suppressed the truth about the Jesus-Magdalene union by smearing her reputation and belittling her as a prostitute.

Not only do we have such popular resurrections of old scripts, but, hints the press and some ideologues, the apocryphal gospels really reveal an earlier and freer form of Christianity that was egalitarian, feminist, and structureless. In contrast, the canonical gospels represent a highly censored and patriarchal form of Christianity that supposedly suppressed the freedom of the earlier forms.

Elaine Pagels wrote a very popular book that voices these sentiments, titled *Beyond Belief: The Secret Gospel of Thomas*. The public ate it up while the scholars correctly pointed out its silliness and its uncritical swallowing of the Gnostic message in Thomas that echoes the New Age doctrine that claims we all have this marvelous spark of divinity in us and that Jesus, a really admirable human being, encourages us to trust in seeking our own truth on the way to salvation ("I am god!" to quote Shirley MacLaine running along the beach). Only a mean-spirited Constantine and his episcopal minions squelched this ever-so nice Jesus movement by introducing creeds and the notion that Jesus is the only way to salvation (this accusation appears again in Brown, as noted below). In short, the Gnostic message in the Gospel of Thomas, ready-made for moderns, is the real gospel.

"Nonsense" is the only responsible response. The fact is that these apocryphal gospels, while occasionally giving us an authentic saying not preserved in the canonical gospels (such as in the Gospel of Thomas), provide no biographical information about Jesus that we do not already know from the canonical gospels. The apocryphal gospels are, in fact, highly imaginative stories that ratchet up the storytelling impulse. They are much like the "texts" of an evolving Santa Claus saga in that they try to fill in what the gospels do not tell us. And that's understandable.

Of course, it's interesting to speculate why the early Church did not include some of the apocryphal gospels in the canon, outside of the out and out heretical ones. Sure, some things in them are spurious or later medieval additions, but the same could be said about some of the canonical gospels. After all, if we kept the accounts of the flight into Egypt, the catching of a fish out of whose mouth miraculously was found a shekel to pay the temple tax (very Grimm Brothers like), the temptation in the desert, and the zapping of the fig tree, why could we not have tolerated the miracles of the child Jesus making birds out of clay or having the palm tree bend over so his mother could gather some fruit, accounts which appear in the apocryphal gospels?

The reason there is interest in the apocryphal gospels is that we are simply not satisfied with the lacunae of the gospel. We always want to know more details: "Who was that masked man?" Who were Mary's parents? What were the names of the three kings? (See, already the unnumbered magi from the East have become three and they, like a made-over Eliza Doolittle, are royalty! A classic example of storytelling at work.) We sense the gospel stories are incomplete, lacking in details that we so dearly want to know but which were apparently uninteresting to the evangelists. So the imaginative apocryphal gospels come to the rescue and supply our storytelling need.

The Interpretative Story

Before we proceed with another example, let me take time to mention the third and final thing we might remember; that often these legendary stories are actually rooted to the biblical text. To understand this, we have to do a little research.

One thing we must know when we pick up the Bible is that the ancients, without exception, were absolutely, totally, and unwaveringly convinced that the Scriptures were cryptic. That is, the text always had two meanings: the literal one and a hidden, deeper meaning. That's because the written biblical text was not essentially a record book of the past but a record written for our benefit now in the present; in other words, what does the text have to say to us today? What does it teach us?

We saw something of this when Christian writers like the evangelists found hidden meanings to Jesus in those ancient Hebrew texts that, on the surface, had no such reference. We see how this conviction flourishes today in all of the Bible Code and end-time books, whose authors claim to have found the key that unlocks the hidden meanings. So there are hidden meanings in Scripture and, from the beginning, interpreters sought them out. In fact, as we have seen, some interpretations have become so standard, so taken for granted, that they have been read as the "natural" meaning. Interpreting the snake in the garden of Eden as Satan is such a case, although the text itself makes no such identification. If you didn't have the time-honored interpretation of some ancient interpreter whose version became sacrosanct, you would not easily make that connection.

Another challenge for the interpreters was how to interpret hard-to-understand texts, contradictory versions, obsolete words, or simply how to flesh out vague commands. Keep the sabbath is one thing, but what does "keeping" involve? Older Catholics might remember that "keeping the sabbath" meant going to church and performing no servile work on Sunday—and servile work, in turn, had to be interpreted (was sewing considered servile work?). So in this and other matters, the ancient interpreters had their work cut out for them, and they did it creatively. Here is a case in point: the text says,

> When Enoch had lived sixty-five years, he became the father of Methuselah. Enoch walked with God after the birth of Methuselah three hundred years, and had other sons and daughters. Thus all the days of Enoch were three hundred sixty-five years. Enoch walked with God; then he was no more, because God took him. (Gen 5:21–24)

The text says Enoch walked with God after the birth of Methuselah. So the interpreters concluded that he didn't before the birth of Methuselah, which in turn clearly means (to some interpreter at least) that at one time he was a sinner who repented after his son's birth. Conclusion: Enoch becomes a model of repentance, so much so that, about five hundred years later, we find this interpretation canonized in the book of Sirach: "Enoch pleased the Lord and was taken up, an example of repentance to all generations" (Sir 44:16). This shows how an interpretation of a biblical text finally *became* a biblical text. Sirach truly thought this was divine revelation, the only true and obvious meaning of the passage from Genesis, and he took it whole.

The point is that ancient interpreters, trying to make a difficult passage intelligible or an embarrassing one more palatable, came up with some creative solutions. For example, the Wisdom of Solomon says that even though it's written in Exodus that the Hebrews "plundered" the Egyptians (Ex 12:36) it wasn't really thievery; the Hebrews were really only collecting back wages they should have received.

Or when Mark writes that the faithless apostles fell asleep three times in the garden while Jesus agonized and came back three times to chastise them—"Could you not keep awake one hour?" (14:37)—Luke, writing years later and not wishing to put the now-older apostles in a bad light, writes, "When he got up from prayer, he came to the disciples and found them sleeping because of grief." (22:45). Poor things! All worn out with grief. Remember how the two nervy apostles, James and John, ask Jesus for places of honor at his right and left—at least that's the way Mark tells it (10:35–40)? A few decades later Matthew removes the embarrassment by having the brothers' mother make the request (20:20–23)!

My point is that some of the interpretations became somewhat wild and fantastical; eventually, some of them took on the character of legends. And people who received them as legends tended to see them only and entirely as that and so dismissed them. These are the skeptics, who feel this way because they forget or, more likely, never knew, the exegetical connection. That is, they read the legends separate from their original biblical roots. But if you take the legends and once more rejoin them to the Bible accounts, they then come across as an imaginative but credible interpretation of the biblical text and don't have to be dismissed out of hand. Once the legends are seen as interpretations with roots in Scripture, stories can be seen in the same way.

Let's go back to the apocryphal gospel of James for an example. This gospel especially has been highly influential in giving us lots of imaginative lore that has been enshrined in much of our art as well as in Christian legend. This is the gospel that provides us with the names of Mary's parents, Joachim and Anne, presents Joseph as an elderly man who carried a lily in his hand (the result of his staff blossoming as a sign that he was picked to be Mary's husband), and even has Mary, at an early age, being presented in the Temple and then living there. Well, none of that is true as we understand truth.

For example, Mary as a young female would never have been presented in the Temple, much less live there. But now try attaching the legend of Mary to its biblical roots and you will see the story in a different light. Remember, the gospel of Luke has already said that Mary was "favored" (Lk 1:38) long before the angel's visit. That is, she was bowed to God's will from an early age, was his "handmaid" long before Gabriel's appearance. In other words, she was dedicated to God from her earliest years and so the story of her presentation in the temple is an imaginative way to make that point. It's a classic example of not reading the text literally but metaphorically or imaginatively.

See how story works? Of course, the trouble is that the conservatives get hung up on the legend and make it an objective tenet of faith, and if you deny that Mary entered the Jewish equivalent of a convent at the age of twelve, you are a heretic, one of those "cafeteria Catholics." The liberals, on the other hand, dismiss the legend altogether with a superior air, but they fail to see and appreciate the story as a truth-telling interpretation of the gospel.

An Addendum to This Chapter

Because of the continuing success of Dan Brown's novel, *The Da Vinci Code*—some 60 million copies at this writing plus, as I mentioned, a motion picture in the works and a report that Brown is working on a sequel—it might be helpful to the reader to add a very brief critique of this work since it touches on Scripture. Most know the plot of the book: Jesus was not divine but a very human young Galilean who married Mary Magdalene. They had a child, and one of their descendants, a young woman, is alive today. The Church suppressed altogether the memory of Mary Magdalene who, after her husband, Jesus, was killed, lived out her life in southern France. Her descendants—Jesus' descendants—are none other than the Merovingian royal family.

These secrets were preserved, however, by a secret society called the Priory of Sion. A bishop, head of the equally secretive Opus Dei, sends one of his acolytes, a reformed killer, to destroy the evidence guarded by the Priory. In his so-called "fact page" in front of the novel, Brown tells us that this Priory of Sion, a European secret society founded in 1099, is a real organization. In 1975, he says, the national library in Paris discovered parchments known as the Secret Dossiers, which identify members of the Priory of Sion, including such luminaries as Isaac Newton, Botticelli, Victor Hugo, and Leonardo Da Vinci.

Leonardo da Vinci, however, slipped the secret knowledge into his painting of the Last Supper when he, in code, gave a clue to the identity of the real Holy Grail—hence the book's title. You see, the Holy Grail, "holy blood," of legendary fame (most recently seen in one of the Indiana Jones movie series), sought after throughout the centuries was actually not a physical cup but rather, Mary Magdalene herself! She was the "chalice," the "vessel" that held Christ's blood, his bloodline, that is, his children. According to Brown, she is clearly the feminine-looking figure Da Vinci painted to Jesus' right, the one we always thought was the apostle John.

But it doesn't stop there. Brown goes on to declare that, hundreds of years after Jesus lived, the emperor Constantine collated the Bible and solemnly declared that only the four canonical gospels were divinely inspired. His purpose was to suppress some eighty apocryphal gospels and "thousands" of other texts that allegedly emphasized Jesus' human traits, which would have formed the basis for his marriage. In other words, Brown is implying that in the early days of Christianity, Jesus was considered just a human moral teacher; it was only some 300 years later that this was assessment was suppressed and Jesus was made divine. This supposed censorship of the other gospels and declaration of Jesus' divinity took place in 325 at the Council of Nicea in a "relatively close vote," to quote the book.

Where to start critiquing all this fantasy? Let me list some facts. First of all, there never was a "Priory of Sion." Brown garnered that information, like most of the assumptions in his novel, almost completely and exclusively from other works such as *Holy Blood Holy Grail*; *The Templar Revelation*; and *The Woman With the Alabaster Jar*. The Priory of Sion has been shown to be a fraud, one originated by a reactionary, anti-Semitic Frenchman in the 1950s. There never was a Priory of Sion. Brown somehow neglects to inform us that the documents found in the Paris library which "proved" its existence and listed its members are bogus. So much for that.

Second, that "relatively close vote" declaring Jesus divine was actually 300 to 2, which is hardly close. The issue at hand was not determining the divinity of Jesus, but the philosophical and theological question of whether he was created or eternal.

Third, the belief in Jesus' divinity was intact and testified to in many of the New Testament writings some three hundred years before Constantine and his cronies. Three-fourths of what is now called the New Testament was considered divinely inspired by the end of the first century. Jesus' divinity was decidedly not a later novelty; Constantine and the Council Fathers did not invent his divinity.

Fourth, there are not thousands of other texts about Jesus. There are fifteen or twenty beyond the four canonical gospels, and very, very few are linked to the apostles.

Fifth, there is no evidence at all that Jesus was married. While it was unusual for a Jewish man not to be married it was not unheard of. There was, as we mention elsewhere in this book, an entire community of Jewish celibates among the Essenes who lived near the Dead Sea; their famous Dead Sea Scrolls attest to this. Professor Karen King of Harvard Divinity School, who has written two books on Mary Magdalene, gets it right. She says that even if it were theoretically possible that Jesus was married—and the gospel accounts, she reminds us, are silent on this point—no evidence exists in biblical or apocryphal works of that period.

Six, the figure next to Jesus in Da Vinci's Last Supper is not Mary Magdalene, but really the apostle John, who is traditionally pictured beardless as a young and attractive youth. He lived the longest of all the apostles (dying in his nineties, it is said), which is why he is pictured so young. And yes, there is no actual chalice or cup pictured in the celebrated Da Vinci's painting. Dan Brown, the author, seizes on this fact as pointing to Mary Magdalene as the "real" chalice or vessel of blood. Actually, we should note that Da Vinci is picturing John's gospel account of the Last Supper. John's, remember, is the one gospel that does not describe the institution of the Eucharist, and the Last Supper is not specified as a Passover meal. Hence, logically, there would be no central chalice of any kind.

Finally, Mary Magdalene has indeed been sometimes confused with the "scarlet woman" who washed Jesus' feet, and so she unfairly had a reputation as a prostitute. This was not a deliberate act on the part of the Church, but a misunderstanding of the biblical text. She does not represent the "sacred feminine" suppressed and demonized by a chauvinistic, male-dominated Church. On the contrary, the Orthodox Christians call her "Equal to the Apostles." Remember, in the gospels hers is the only name to appear in each of the lists of the women disciples, and her name is always listed first. The Risen Christ directed Magdalene to bring the news of the resurrection to the disciples, and so the early Christian writers celebrated her as the "apostle to the apostles." Church Fathers like Hippolytus, Gregory the Great, and Leo the Great variously sang her praises as "the apostle of the apostles," "the representative of the church," and "the new Eve announcing not death but life." Not to mention that over forty years ago the Church officially titled her as an apostle in its liturgical calendar.

So much for *The Da Vinci Code*, a hodgepodge of speculation, inaccuracies, and innuendo. If you look for it in the library or in a bookstore, you'll find it in the fiction section. And that's just what it is: a good story, perhaps, but fiction nonetheless.

I have my own thoughts about why this book is so enormously popular; for what they're worth, here they are.

1. It's a darn good read and that alone goes a long way.

2. The book taps into our love of conspiracies and intrigue; both elements are there aplenty.

3. For anti-Catholics, the book and its plot confirm what they have always believed: that the Catholic Church is wicked, devious, and power-hungry.

4. The timing of the book's appearance was perfect. With its heavy accent on secrecy, it appeared at the very moment of the Church's cover-up over the sex abuse scandal, making the book's plot seem more plausible than ever.

5. The book depicts Jesus as sexually active, something mighty pleasing for a culture that glorifies sexual activity and has little use for celibacy.

6. The book resonates with feminists who rightly want to challenge female suppression by a largely male Church hierarchy, and the anti-woman bias evident in the Mediterranean cultural tone of the Bible.

10.

BIBLICAL EXPANSIONS

S tories, by nature expand. As an example, let's take a look at two unique biblical passages: Deuteronomy 26:4–9 and Nehemiah 9:6–24. What makes these passages unique is that both are creeds, or confessions, recited on ritual occasions. These creeds are the core of Israel's identity, just as the Nicene Creed, which we recite at liturgy, defines who we are and what we believe as Christians. Now note several things about these basic, self-identifying creeds. First, they are separated by many, many centuries. The Deuteronomy creedal statement goes back, perhaps, to 1200 BC; the Nehemiah creed goes back to third or fourth century BC. So you have some eight or nine hundred years between these two creeds, and you know they're not going to stay static. So let's see what happened to them as time went by. (Hint: storytelling inevitably took place). Listen to Deuteronomy:

When the priest takes the basket from your hand and sets it

down before the altar of the Lord your God, you shall make this response before the Lord your God [note the ritual setting]: "A wandering Aramean was my ancestor; he went down into Egypt and lived there as an alien, few in number, and there he became a great nation, mighty and populous. When the Egyptians treated us harshly and afflicted us, by imposing hard labor on us, we cried to the Lord, the God of our ancestors; the Lord heard our voice and saw our affliction, our toil, and our oppression. The Lord brought us out of Egypt with a mighty hand and an outstretched arm, with a terrifying display of power, and with signs and wonders; and he brought us into this place and gave us this land, a land flowing with milk and honey."

That's it. This is what was you were supposed to say on the most important ritual day of the year. This is what defined you as a member of the chosen race. Notice there are three basic beliefs to this identity. The first is that God chose a patriarch. Be careful here: this is not Abraham as you automatically think since you are influenced by the later creed. This is Jacob, who was an Aramean. So at the beginning of Israel's story stands Jacob; Abraham and Isaac are not even mentioned. The second theme is the bondage in Egypt and the Exodus, and the third theme is the conquest of Canaan. That's it: this is the most important, three-fold creedal summary of what makes you an Israelite: God chose Jacob, we were burdened in Egypt and freed by Yahweh, and the Lord gave us this land.

Now compare this to the saga written by Nehemiah some eight or nine hundred years later (9:6–24):

Ezra said: "You are the Lord, you alone; you have made heaven, the heaven of heavens, with all their host, the earth and all that is on it, the seas and all that is in them. To all of them you give life, and the host of heaven worships you. You are the Lord, the God who chose Abram and brought him out of Ur of the Chaldeans and gave him the name Abraham; and you found his heart faithful before you, and made with him a covenant to give to his descendants the land of the Canaanite, the Hittite, the Amorite, the Perizzite, the Jebusite, and the Girgashite; and you have fulfilled your promise, for you are righteous.

"And you saw the distress of our ancestors in Egypt and heard their cry at the Red Sea. You performed signs and wonders against Pharaoh and all his servants and all the people of his land, for you knew that they acted insolently against our ancestors. You made a name for yourself, which remains to this day. And you divided the sea before them, so that they passed through the sea on dry land, but you threw their pursuers into the depths, like a stone into mighty waters. Moreover, you led them by day with a pillar of cloud, and by night with a pillar of fire, to give them light on the way in which they should go. You came down also upon Mount Sinai, and spoke with them from heaven, and gave them right ordinances and true laws, good statutes and commandments, and you made known your holy sabbath to them and gave them commandments and statutes and a law through your servant Moses. For their hunger you gave them bread from heaven, and for their thirst you brought water for them out of the rock, and you told them to go in to possess the land that you swore to give them.

"But they and our ancestors acted presumptuously and stiffened their necks and did not obey your commandments; they refused to obey, and were not mindful of the wonders that you performed among them; but they stiffened their necks and determined to return to their slavery in Egypt. But you are a God ready to forgive, gracious and merciful, slow to anger and abounding in steadfast love, and you did not forsake them. Even when they had cast an image of a calf for themselves and said, 'This is your God who brought you up out of Egypt,' and had committed great blasphemies, you in your great mercies did not forsake them in the wilderness; the pillar of cloud that led them in the way did not leave them by day, nor the pillar of fire by night that gave them light on the way by which they should go. You gave your good spirit to instruct them, and did not withhold your manna from their mouths, and gave them water for their thirst. Forty years you sustained them in the wilderness so that they lacked nothing; their clothes did not wear out and their feet did not swell. And you gave them kingdoms and peoples, and allotted to them every corner, so they took possession of the land of King Sihon of Heshbon and the land of King Og of Bashan. You multiplied their descendants like the stars of heaven, and brought them into the land that you had told their ancestors to enter and possess. So the descendants went in and possessed the land, and you subdued before them the inhabitants of the land."

That's a long passage and what a contrast to the passage from Deuteronomy! Both are creeds; both are confessions. This is what you are expected to say in a ritual setting to declare who you are. But what an expansion of the story! Take a look. The Nehemiah creed contains five themes, not three. The first theme is creation, which is not even mentioned in the Deuteronomy creed because being an Israelite, it's assumed you confess that God made heaven and earth. It took some nine hundred years for there to be a need to mention that creation is attributed to the God of Israel.

Second, according to Nehemiah, the patriarchal period begins with Abraham, then Isaac, and finally, Jacob. The story has not only been expanded to include Abraham and Isaac, but has been expanded to make these three figures relatives, which is a common way of linking separate folklores. So here in Nehemiah, Israel's story begins with Jacob's grandfather, his son, and his grandson and we get fairly elaborate stories about each of them.

Third, both creeds mention the bondage in Egypt and the Exodus, but in Nehemiah you have the kind of fabulous additional details that would make Cecil B. DeMille salivate. In Deuteronomy, we were enslaved and Yahweh saved us, period. In Nehemiah, the sea was split, Yahweh stretched out his arms, and walls of dry land formed on the left and on the right. There was a cloud by day, a pillar of fire by night, water that didn't run out and feet that stayed in good shape. All of these details are absent in the Deuteronomy account.

Fourth, in Deuteronomy it is simply stated that the Israelites go directly into Canaan. But Nehemiah adds a totally new tradition, saying that the Israelites wandered into the desert, where a leader named Moses goes to Mount Sinai and receives the Torah. Deuteronomy makes no mention of Moses, of Sinai, or of the Torah. Today, you can't tell the story of the Exodus without mentioning Moses. But Deuteronomy 26 did. There is no mention of Moses at all.

The fifth theme in Nehemiah, as in Deuteronomy, is the conquest of Canaan.

Now notice this further: Nehemiah's schema becomes the pattern for the Hebrew Scriptures and determines the order of the Pentateuch, the first five books of the Hebrew Scriptures. When the Hebrew Scriptures was being organized, it followed the story not as it was told in the oral tradition but as it came to be in the written tradition. Thus the Bible, like Nehemiah's creed, starts with creation even though Genesis is not the first written book of the Bible. It's a later book placed first to conform to Nehemiah's schema. The Pentateuch ends with the entrance into the Promised Land, following Nehemiah's outline.

What is going on here is what happens to all national (and even personal) stories; namely, stories get rearranged and stories expand. We all know that. Think of family stories that have been expanded over the years.

The Bible as we know it is the expanded, orderly recording of an early tradition that formed over eight or nine centuries. The point I'm making is that in the period between both confessional creeds, between that nine hundred years, Nehemiah introduces brand new material and greatly elaborates on the old previous material. That's the law of living stories. Details have been added to underscore and highlight the significance of the event and the forbearance of Yahweh for his Chosen People, but the core tradition of slavery, choseness, and deliverance remains.

Those Fabled Patriarchs

All this should give us a handle on the patriarchs, Abraham, Isaac, Jacob, Moses, David, and others. Among certain archaeologists and scholars, there is real doubt that any of them existed (except David). They and their exploits are folkloric constructs, disguised copies of Near East mythological figures. There were some historical tribal figures whose lives did, in fact, correspond to those of the patriarchs, but the local lore about them inflated into a national, biblical account. Still, from a storytelling point of view, that they may have arisen from folklore and legend need not negate these people altogether. Scripture scholar Raymond Brown gives us a good perspective:

> Suppose I were to ask you whether you really think that Washington cut down the cherry tree, or threw a coin across the Potomac, or slept in all the houses in which he is supposed to have bivouacked, you might answer, "Well, I think some of that is legend." How would you then reply if I said to you, "Well, if you begin doubting those things about Washington, how do you know that Lincoln led the Union to victory over the Confederacy, or that Teddy Roosevelt presided over the building of the Panama Canal?" You would soon be forced to recognize that there are different bodies of evidence for different claims and that at times stories about some people are told with a certain legendary atmosphere whereas stories about others are unadornedly factual.

> The same has to be recognized in the stories associated with the great biblical characters. King Arthur, King William the Conqueror (responsible for the Norman invasion of England), and Queen Elizabeth II are all monarchs associated with British history; but the quality of what we know about each runs the gamut from allegory with some historical details in the case of Arthur, to a general but often not

specific history in the case of William the Conqueror, and finally to the ability to construct almost a day-by-day account of the activities of Elizabeth II.

So also, the stories pertinent to Abraham have a general historical setting; but he is presented as the father of two peoples, Israel and Ishmael (the Arabs), so there is a somewhat allegorical character to the story. The story of Moses is part of a national epic in which the achievements of the individual and the history of a people are blended. Parts of the story of David probably stem from a court biographer who lived in that period of history and wrote fairly factually. There is history in all three narratives, but varying amounts of history and of detail (*101 Questions and Answers on the Bible*).

And so there is a core tradition with lots of storied details.

Before we end this discussion, let me share another allied storytelling principle: stories interpret events in the light of available symbols. For instance, the evangelists, as we have seen, read the Old Testament as a source for prophesying about Jesus. To our minds, they then made some off-the-wall applications that the texts themselves did not seem to warrant, unless they were twisted beyond recognition. But the evangelists were only doing what we would do: using common symbols available at hand and applying them in a creative way. You may have noticed that in these pages I made references to Columbo, George Washington, Barney Fife, and so on. Is there anybody on the planet who doesn't know who these real and fictional people are? In trying to explain myself I leaned on common symbols and lore, bending them to my needs, and adding interest to my points.

But this may be a problem in a hundred or five hundred years from now when people will no longer understand these references, and so we'll need decoding commentaries or footnotes to explain them. That's why we have so much trouble with the biblical stories: we have, in some instances, lost the key to their symbols and references. The biblical writers have a linguistic code that is different from ours, one we haven't completely cracked.

11.

THE STORIES
ARE TALL

Biblical stories are classified as "myths" in the sense that they are foundational stories of high imagination. But like all myths, they have a point to make. To this end, the Bible contains, as we have seen, all kinds of mythological material, folklore, and legends along with cultural folk heroes such as Abraham, Isaac, Jacob, Moses, Joshua, and David. Some of these people are quite embarrassing, to the point where you would think the biblical writers wouldn't want to mention them. Abraham, for example, was a trickster, Samson was just plain stupid, and David was a thug, an adulterer, and a murderer. Even so, they are the national heroes of Israel.

Then there are those delightful, fictional short stories—and they are fictional—like the wonderful books of Ruth, Jonah, and Esther. These explore in an interesting and entertaining way how Israel is to relate to its neighbors. For instance, in the Book of

Ruth, Ruth is a Moabite, a foreigner, one of the traditional enemies of Israel. But what do you know? She turns out to be pretty
decent. In fact, she becomes the grandmother of King David and
an ancestress of Jesus. So maybe the story is saying that Israel
need not be so self-centered, that goodness exists elsewhere.
Jonah is sent to Israel's worst enemy, Assyria, and these scum
repent. So maybe, the story suggests, one's enemies are worthy of
kindness and capable of reconciliation. Then too we find in the
Bible those fictional court tales, like the books of Esther and
Daniel, which basically provide instruction to the Jews on how to
live and retain their identity in the diaspora, as captives in a foreign land of foreign gods.

And so the Bible is not necessarily an historical record. For
example, it is doubtful, according to scholars, that Jerusalem was
David's capital city, for in his time it was just a small hovel. It is
certain, as we have noted before, that Joshua did not bring down
the walls of Jericho because the archaeological evidence shows
that by the time Joshua arrived Jericho was already a ruined city.

As a classic example of non-history, let's go back and take a
look at the exotic book of Genesis, which contains all kinds of
cosmological myths or "myths of origin." Like all ancient and
modern peoples, the Hebrews wanted to know, how did the
world get started? Why are we here? Who created the world?
What are we supposed to be doing with our lives? These are
urgent and timeless questions, and myth tries to deal with them
in roundabout, imaginative language within its time and culture.
Israel's myths, for example, are clearly written in dialogue with—
sometimes in competition with—the other Near East myths of
Babylon, Assyria, and Egypt. As such it tries to define itself in
relation to its neighbors, as well as over and against its neighbors.

Thus chapter 1 of Genesis is not a factual story of creation,
much less a literal, scientific explanation of the origins of the uni-
verse. Rather, it is a myth; that is, an identity story, a meaning
story, a community story, an ethical story. To appreciate it you
must realize that Genesis 1 is specifically a response over and

against the Babylonian creation myth called Enu Elish. The Babylonian myth begins with the words "when in high," and ends with the founding of the Babylonian capital. Note that this is a myth of a conquering kingdom that ends in space, the sacred space of their capital, and it tells the Babylonians who they are.

In contrast, the Hebrew text begins with "When in the beginning..." and ends with God resting on the seventh day, thus the seventh day became hallowed. So what we have here is that the biblical myth talks about time and makes time sacred rather than space. There is a reason for this. Genesis was written by Jews during the sixth century, when they were in exile. At that time they were in captivity in Babylon, and they had no space of their own. So they countered the Babylonian myth which they heard all around them.

The Israelite version, concocted in exile away from the homeland, says, "We don't need to be tied down to a place to know who we are. We have our own God and our own story, and we will privilege time rather than space." This version makes sense when you're in exile. You can make time sacred wherever you are, apart from your own land, your temple, your capital, your physical sacred space. You can keep the sabbath, mark the days, honor the week in a foreign land or anywhere. And so this part of the Genesis story is more than a story of origins. It is an identity story, a story of how people define themselves in the midst of a alien land and culture.

Jacob on the Ropes

For one more example of how biblical stories operate, let's take Jacob, that less than admirable man who tricked his brother Esau out of his inheritance. Go to the famous scene where Jacob is wrestling with God. The bible story—the biblical myth—reports that Jacob is returning home after years spent with his father-in-law, Laban (a shady character if there ever was one), but he fears that he will encounter his brother Esau along the way (as well he might). When Jacob arrives at the river, he has to wrestle with someone, but it's not clear who this is, at first.

In the folklore of the times, river demons who blocked people's journeys were common, and so Jacob is obviously prepared for just such an encounter. (By the way, lest you think that the presence of river gods to be appeased is only a quaint bit of ancient folklore, just remember the last time you threw three coins into the Trevi fountain or a well or a stream. You were unconsciously appeasing the river god!) Anyway, Jacob wrestles with his opponent, who at first seems only a man but in the end is revealed as God. It is at this point that Jacob receives the name "Israel," which means, the text says, "God strives"—although that interpretation is doubtful.

At first glance, then, this story appears to be a biblical myth or meaning story. But on reflection we sense the deeper truth. The point of Jacob wrestling with God is not in the expected sense, that "God strives" on behalf of Israel, but rather that God is striving *against* Israel. In this foundational myth, the descendants of Israel are being taught *not* to think of their God as some happy-faced being who makes them feel good, but rather as one who confronts them in uncomfortable ways. That Jacob is injured in the hip and walks away limping reveals the truth that one does not come away unscathed from an encounter with God.

This story shows that the spiritual journey is filled with resistance. We all wrestle with God a thousand times a day. We question whether God exists at all or where is God in our sickness or loss or trials. In the garden of Gethsemane Jesus wrestled with God: "Father, if it is possible, remove this chalice from me." Is the story of Jacob at the river historical or factual? I don't know; it could be. Is it true? Yes, in the sense of a core truth. Is it a myth? Again, yes, in that it gives Israel its identity and defines the kind of God they worship. And this identity separates them from all others; it sustains them.

Let me bring this same point into the twentieth century. Psychiatrist Robert Coles likes to tell the story of a little girl named Ruby whom he met during the early days of desegregation. Coles became intrigued by the seven-year-old, who had to be escorted to school by federal marshals. She would get out of the car and be met by jeering mobs who shouted racial epithets at her. She would pause, bow her head for a moment, and then walk into the school, staring straight ahead. Coles came to know Ruby's family and finally felt comfortable asking Ruby why she always paused before she went into class. She said, "I'm saying a little prayer. I'm saying, 'Father, forgive them for they know not what they do.'"

This little girl, Ruby, had access to a religious story and tradition, and it gave her great strength. The point? The Calvary story—even if it were not factual but rather interpretative—provided meaning for her personal crucifixion, gave her identity as a Christian, connected her to a community of saints and martyrs, sustained her in time of need, and showed her how to act. In short, it functioned as her meaning story (myth).

The Arts

Consider the idea that story is basically metaphor, a carrier of deeper meanings conveyed through the art of the storyteller's use of exaggeration, symbols, color, details and so on. Perhaps a good analogy to this concept can be found in painting. The artist is dealing with a flat surface and a blank canvas. On it, he or she has to convey invitation, challenge, and meaning by providing symbols that no one takes literally. An easy example of this is the halo that surround the heads of holy people. No one in the world thinks Paul or Joseph or Peter walked around with a spherical light emanating from their heads. Who would want to sit behind them in a movie?

And take a look at the Renaissance portrayals of Mary, all gussied up in elegant satin attire sitting against the background of an Italian villa. Everyone knows Mary isn't Italian and did not live in a Renaissance countryside. But the Italian painter wants to let you know not only that Mary is special (a spiritual queen, a royal personage) and that "all generations are calling her blessed" (the core tradition), but also that she is a woman who transcends time and space: she belongs to all nationalities and all peoples. You can't say enough about her. You can't paint enough about her. Mary, the first and truest disciple of Jesus, deserves the royal best when paint is applied to canvas.

What about angels? They're spirits and therefore invisible. So how do you paint an invisible spirit? You paint them as human beings (so you can see them) but with all kinds of signals to suggest that they are more, such as wings since they, like the god Mercury, swiftly hasten to carry messages between heaven and earth. (Forget the cherubs: those tiny foreshortened shoulder wings could never get those plump infants airborne!)

Heavenly saints wear gold crowns because gold is the one metal that doesn't rust, which conveys that heaven is timeless, eternal. They strum harps because music is the nearest thing to ecstasy we have on earth. And if a saint has an animal at his or her feet, it means something: a lion for Jerome recalls the legend about that beast. A dog at the feet of a crusader says he died abroad. The four evangelists are represented by an eagle, ox, angel, and lion.

And so a work of art is not to be taken literally (even a portrait). It is filled with angles, style, lighting, and symbols that convey more than meets the eye, some deeper truth. Stories, too, are filled with images. Thunder and lightning on Mount Sinai are as much symbols of the divine presence as halos are symbols of inner holiness. They don't exist literally but to tell us something.

The Image Industry

Actually, imagery is not foreign to us moderns. Quite the contrary; we live in a culture what supports a gazillion dollar image industry. "Image is everything" is the slogan. So politicians hire spin doctors to make their words special, and ordinary people who don't want to be ordinary make cosmetic surgery the most popular form of surgery in the United States. A girl with a receding chin and large nose gets a surgical makeover and looks gorgeous. She meets a surgically altered handsome man who once had a receding chin and large nose. Keeping their secrets, they marry and—to their surprise—their baby has a receding chin and large nose! Where did that come from, the parents wonder? No problem. The child will just start earlier on the cosmetic surgery journey. Women are having foot surgery so they can fit into the latest Manolo Blahniks or Jimmy Choos. (I like the New Yorker cartoon that shows a voluptuous blond in a mini-skirt amid a group of sleepy senior citizens sitting in rocking chairs in a nursing home. "It cost a bundle," says the younger looking woman, "but I can't tell you how much better I feel about myself.") ABC captured the whole expansive and expensive image industry in its television series called "Extreme Makeover."

Of course, as someone observed, if everyone in the world has cosmetic surgery in order to look attractive (attractiveness, of course, is a cultural standard that changes from era to era) then no one will look attractive. The point of image enhancement is not to look like everyone else, but to look *better* than everyone else. People build McMansions with fifteen rooms for two or three people in order to impress. Ego drives the Hummer. Large mansions, extravagant cars, brand name coffins (I kid you not) and upscale mausoleums that feature auditoriums, exhibit space for art, waterfalls, and skylights, $700 baby strollers, and $248 jeans are not just consumer hype. They are consumer imagery that says, "Look at me. Everyone can see that I am a Calvin Klein, Armani-suited kind of a guy who knows the right wines, sleeps with right women (with the aid of Viagra, of course), drives a BMW, and takes my winter vacation in the Cayman Islands." This is our image of success!

I write this not just to titillate you but to call to your consciousness just how much we all live by imagery—from the clothes we wear, the hairstyles we sport, the cars we drive, the homes we live in, and the extent to which we consume. They are all "statements," and we are constantly urged to make statements about ourselves—which, of course, can come only from purchasing the right product. With this in mind, let's move back to stories in general, and the Bible stories in particular.

Much of story—indeed its attraction and charm—is in its imagery and in the subtle statements it makes. "It was a dark and stormy night..." immediately sets up an image in our imaginations. (Of course, we first have to overcome our imagery of Snoopy at his typewriter in order to get to Edward Bulwer-Lytton's novel, *Paul Clifford*, which starts with that famous line.) Fundamentally, the condition of the sky has nothing to do with the plot but through suggestive imagery, it portends dark doings. It sets us up, and predisposes our mood and expectations. For the sake of argument, let's say that the night may have been bright and starry, but the author has changed that detail to get to a place that, in reality, was *not* bright and starry: the inner workings of an evil heart. Did he lie? Technically, yes. Storywise and humanwise, no. There was a deeper truth going on beneath the surface subtly suggested by the night imagery.

> On the morning of the third day there was thunder and lightning, as well as a thick cloud on the mountain, and a blast of a trumpet so loud that all the people who were in the camp trembled. Moses brought the people out of the camp to meet God. They took their stand at the foot of the mountain. Now Mount Sinai was wrapped in smoke, because the Lord had descended upon it in fire; the smoke went up like the smoke of a kiln, while the whole mountain shook violently. As the blast of the trumpet grew louder and louder, Moses would speak and God would answer him in thunder (Ex 19:16–19).

Whew! Talk about images. The ancients did not have the technology to do all kinds of Indiana Jones camera tricks, but they *did* have a store of natural images to get their point across.

Whether all that thunder and lightning occurred is really irrelevant. For a people who lived totally bent to nature, these natural phenomena were terrifying and the forceful images were the best they could come up with to fanfare the presence of an all powerful God.

End Note

I just mentioned the lines popularized by Charlie Brown's celebrated dog, Snoopy, "It was a dark and stormy night," taken from the 1830 Bulwer-Lytton novel. You may not know it, but there is an annual "Bulwer-Lytton Fiction Contest" that challenges writers to come up with the opening sentence to the worst of all possible novels. The winner in the year 2003 was a woman named Marian Simms. Her entry is this:

> They had but one last remaining night together, so they embraced each other as tightly as that two-flavor entwined string cheese that is orange and yellowish-white, the orange probably being a bland Cheddar and the white Mozzarella, although it could possibly be Provolone.

That's hilarious and I can't help but think (perhaps unfairly) of some of those people who, incapable of imagination, self-righteously parse the Bible from a literal or rational mentality.

12.

Let's Go
to the Movies

In this chapter, let's take a look at something more familiar to us, a storytelling device that is so common yet so subtle that it works its magic on us without our consciously being aware of it. It is the movie score, the music that accompanies a movie. The more unaware of it we are, the more successful it is.

The score gives us the clues that tell us how to emote and perceive. We know almost immediately, from the opening music, what kind of movie we're about to see: a comedy, a tragedy, science fiction, a romance, and so on. As the villain stalks the unwary victim, the music intensifies; as the car chase goes into high gear, the music beats faster and louder; as the moment of revelation takes place, the music swells; as the waves sweep over the lifeboat the music pounds.

But notice how conditioned we are not to ask the logical question: where are the musicians? There's no sixty-piece orchestra in the lifeboat or the bedroom or the scary alley. We know that. Intellectually, we know that somewhere in a recording studio an orchestra is dubbing in the sound as the players watch the movie. We know that literally there was no music during the events in the picture any more than there were halos encircling holy heads. We accept the music for what it is: a symbol, a storyteller's (director's) trick to suggest the action or mood. It is, in the last analysis, a storytelling device. It exists to enhance the core story, to guide and move the audience's emotions. (I always imagine strict biblical fundamentalists dealing with this by saying that all the orchestra players are midgets and they are really in the theatre— only you don't see them.)

While we're on the subject, you can catch some of the creativity of the biblical storyteller by listening to the words of the movie storyteller, namely, the director. Here, for example, is Sidney Lumet who directed such well-regarded films as *Twelve Angry Men*, *Long Day's Journey into Night*, *The Pawnbroker*, *Serpico*, *Murder on the Orient Express*, *Network*, and others. He wrote a book called, not surprisingly, *Making Movies* (which ought to be required reading for any Scripture course). Listen to his words as if they were spoken, say, by one of the evangelists:

> Now comes the most important decision I have to make: What is this movie about? I'm not talking about plot, although in certain very good melodramas the plot is all they're about. And that's not bad. A good, rousing, scary story can be a hell of a lot of fun. But what is it about emotionally? What is the theme of the movie, the spine, the arc [the core tradition]? What does the movie mean to me? Personalizing the movie is very important. I'm going to be working flat out for the next six, nine, twelve months. The picture had better have some meaning to me. Otherwise, the physical labor (very hard indeed) will become twice as exhausting. The word "meaning" can spread over a very wide range. The question "What is this movie about?" will be asked over and over again throughout the book. For now,

suffice it to say that the theme (the what of the movie) is going to determine the style (the how of the movie).

The theme will decide the specifics of every selection made in all the following chapters. I work from the inside out. What the movie is about will determine how it will be cast, how it will look, how it will be edited, how it will be musically scored, how it will be mixed, how the titles will look, and, with a good studio, how it will be released. What it's about will determine how it is to be made....

Once we've agreed on the all-important question "What's this picture about?" we can start in on the details. First comes an examination of each scene in sequence, of course. Does this scene contribute to the overall theme? How? Does it contribute to the story line? To character? Is the story line moving in an ever increasing arc of tension or drama ? In the case of a comedy, is it getting funnier? Is the story being moved forward by the characters? In a good drama, the line where characters and story blend should be indiscernible.

To illustrate his words, I must interject a scene from one of my favorite movies: Alfred Hitchcock's *North by Northwest*. Remember that famous scene in which Cary Grant is alone in the Kansas plains? Suddenly a double-wing duster plane comes out of nowhere to strafe him with bullets. Storyteller Hitchcock wanted to convey the utter loneliness and remoteness of the place in order to pursue his favorite theme (what we might call the core story or tradition): no matter where you are, no matter how safe you think you are, no matter if you're in the middle of nowhere (as Cary Grant was), evil will get you. Of course, long ago Shakespeare harbored the same notion, only he put it more elegantly:

Swift as a shadow, short as any dream;
Brief as the lightning in the collied night,
That in a spleen unfolds heaven and earth,
And ere man hath power to say, "Behold!"
The jaws of darkness do devour it up:

So quick bright things come to confusion.

To convey this "truth," Hitchcock turned off the soundtrack completely and simply panned the camera slowly in all four directions showing nothing but miles and miles of empty land. All is utter, eerie stillness—until evil roars in. The truly great movies like *Gone with the Wind*, *Citizen Kane*, *On the Waterfront*, *Driving Miss Daisy*, resonate in our souls because they, like Hitchcock's movies, provide striking metaphors and symbols that probe deeper than the surface. We think about these movies for a long time after we've seen them.

On the other hand, poor movies are all on the surface. That, by the way, is the basic critique of pornographic movies: they are flat, linear productions with no metaphors, symbols, or invitations to depth. What you see is what you get and what you get is what you see: all image. And that's the way the producers and audiences want it. The men or women are reduced to consumable, replaceable commodities utterly beyond all personal relationships. Surface, sensation, image, and slickness are all that count. There is no more to life is the message.

Back to Sidney Lumet:

Making a movie has always been about telling a story. Some movies tell a story and leave you with a feeling. Some movies tell a story and leave you with a feeling and give you an idea. Some tell a story, leave you with a feeling, give you an idea and reveal something about yourself and others. And surely the way you tell that story should relate somehow to what that story is.

Evangelists in the Director's Chair

Lumet's words make a pretty good mission statement for the biblical writers. They're a good summary of what faced, say, the evangelists Matthew, Mark, Luke, and John—the four sacred movie directors, if you will. What is the Jesus story about? What does it mean? How will that meaning determine the style? How will it be cast?

Art, music, movies: they are all in the realm of storytelling. By way of illustration, let's look at the storytelling art (core tradition + creative details) in reference to Jesus' passion, the oldest core tradition written down. There is, for example, John's use of the "split screen," a technique he uses often. The woman at the well is on one screen telling her townsfolk about the man she met who told her her life . At the same time, on the other screen, Jesus speaks to his disciples. Or, on one screen Jesus is professing his faith before Pilate, while simultaneously Peter is denying his faith on another. As Judas leaves to betray Jesus, it is John who tells us, "Now it was night." Did he mean "night" in the sense that the day is over, or "night" in the sense that Judas' heart was black with a dastardly deed being born?

Or consider the use of the mystical number three in the carefully crafted "camera" choreography found in the story of the Garden of Gethsemane. In this dramatic scene, Jesus moves in three stages. One, he is separated from the main body of his disciples. Two, he is separated from the three he took with him (Peter, James, and John). Three, he now goes alone to face death. This detailed, three-step movement dramatizes the core truth of Jesus' abandonment and utter aloneness. Then John returns three times to Jesus' disciples, yet each time Jesus finds no assistance from them. Notice the creative technique use of three: rejected three times! Moving in three stages towards a lonely death. This device makes the scene both poignant and memorable.

The pattern of three is well established even in our own time. Many of our jokes use this device. There is always a Franciscan, a Dominican, and a Jesuit; or an Italian, a Pole, and a Jew. Two is not enough to establish contrast; four is too many, too complicated. Three is just right for dramatic purposes. Think of what Glinda said to Dorothy: Just click your heels three times!

So it is in the passion narratives: three disciples, three times Jesus goes back. In Mark the disciples fall asleep three times, Peter denies Jesus three times, Peter professes three times, Pilate declares Jesus innocent three times, Mark uses the hours of three, six, and nine as a frame for his narrative. Even in our devotional tradition, in the stations of the cross, how many times does Jesus fall? Three!

How about this? Why did Jesus take Peter, James, and John with him into the Garden of Gethsemane?

> He took with him Peter and James and John, and began to be distressed and agitated. And he said to them, "I am deeply grieved, even to death; remain here, and keep awake." (Mark 14:33–34)

But why Peter, James, and John? Because they are the only ones of the disciples who said they would not fail! Peter promised that he would never deny Jesus; James and John asked for places on Jesus' right and left, and said that they could and would drink of his chalice. Jesus' choice of these three disciples is unsettling detail used in the passion story to warn those whose words are stronger than their action.

A story is verbal art. Like all art there is more there than meets the eye (or ear). It's more than a simple tale. Story tells you more on a deeper level than what the surface words imply. Thus stories should not be read (heard) literally but symbolically (and even straightforward, literal, dry, official, scientific, objective prose betrays an attitude, mindset, mentality, and philosophy of life). No matter how wild a story may seem, we must respect the fact that somewhere behind the exorbitant language and fantastic imagery there's some truth trying to be told and people trying to be formed by what is being told.

This principle may also give us a handle on those terribly sadistic passages where Yahweh orders genocide and mass murder. Such words were not spoken by God but put there by the story-teller-writer to make a point, expressed in the only cultural way he knew how. That point is that God is indeed sovereign, that God has a plan, that God has a will and desire to befriend Israel and through it, the whole human race. Nothing must get in the way of Yahweh's inexorable love. This thought is expressed by a primitive people through stories of violence that reflect the relentless drive to see that Yahweh's yearnings—"You are my people, I am your God"—will be, must be, fulfilled. So putting women and children to the sword and dashing babies' heads against rocks is the culturally primitive storyteller's version of "Thy will be done." It's horribly gruesome and crude by our standards but still within the boundaries of a melting wicked witch (the *Wizard of Oz*), a giant smashing to earth by the ax of an enterprising lad (*Jack and the Beanstalk*), and a wolf brutally beheaded before it could swallow up the promise and fulfillment of a young girl (*Little Red Riding Hood*). Which brings us to our next topic.

A Nice Aside

This spinoff might seem a bit off our subject, but not by too much; that is, the role of fairy tales. In recent times these were mistakenly thought to have been created for children and were confined to their domain. Yet nothing could be further from the truth. From the very beginning, fairy tales were tales of hope for adults in the face of the harshness, unfairness, and mysteries of life. They existed to humanize barbaric forces beyond people's control by offering powerful metaphors to conquer them. For example: to children, adults are giants who daily impose their will on lesser creatures—like children; but a clever kid named Jack can get the better of adults any day. The dynamics of fairy tales and story (including the biblical stories) are the same. Both are oral-aural exercises written down on paper and are always best heard (read) aloud and performed. As the intrepid and brilliant transcriber of fairy tales, Laura Gonzenbach, wrote to a friend:

> Now I'd like to tell you that I've done my best to write down the tales exactly as they were told to me. However, I've not been able to recapture exactly the genuine charm of these tales that lies in the manner and way the tales are told by these Sicilian women. Most of them tell the tales in a lively fashion by acting out the entire plot with their hands, making very expressive gestures. While talking, they even stand up and walk around the room when it's appropriate. They

never use "he says" because they change the people's voices always through intonation (*Beautiful Angiola: The Great Treasury of Sicilian Folk and Fairy Tales Collected by Laura Gonzenbach*).

You can almost see these Sicilian ladies in action. And remember, they are Mediterranean women and this is exactly the way the Bible stories were originally performed, not merely told.

Fairy tales are heavily symbolic and metaphorical and therefore, are imaginative ways of encountering truth. As Melanie McDonagh puts it:

> Fairy tales, the ones we know best, have always seemed to me to be fundamentally Christian. It's hard to think of many that don't echo the spirit of the Magnificat, in the exaltation of the humble and the casting down of the proud. It's the runt of the litter who comes up trumps in these stories, the youngest brother, the daughter displaced by the arrival of the stepmother, the widow's only son. And it's especially true of the stories of Grimm. Tom Thumb is too small to notice, but he takes on an ogre; Cinderella shows how the last shall be first and the first last (*Tablet*, December, 2000).

In his book *Orthodoxy*, G.K. Chesterton has a chapter called "The Ethics of Elfland," in which he explains the spiritual wisdom found in stories such as *Jack and the Beanstalk, Cinderella, Beauty and the Beast,* and *Sleeping Beauty.* C.S. Lewis, George MacDonald, and J.R.R. Tolkein all pointed out the religious underpinnings of fairy tales. Since the movie versions came out, Tolkein's *Lord of the Rings* series has achieved cult status. It is, as the author said, "a fundamentally religious and Catholic work," the classic tale of the human journey. Andrew Krivak writes:

> From the tradition of Christian narrative, *The Lord of the Rings* absorbs the elements of the journey of the heart. Consider, for instance, the Gospel of St. Luke, Augustine's *Confessions,* and Dante's *Divine Comedy.* Here the journey loses neither its emphasis on conflict nor its sense of

urgency and departure, but the path—either of return or of no return—leads through a spiritual as well as a geographical landscape. The story of Luke's gospel is Jesus' journey from Bethlehem to Jerusalem, the journey from birth to death, and from crucifixion to resurrection. In the *Confessions* Augustine's journey becomes the part of the heart that is "restless until it rests in God." For Dante in the *Divine Comedy*, the poet is the man lost midway in life in the tangled forests of sin, his hope nearly "abandoned," except for the guide who leads him through the tortures of hell so that he may redirect his vision to the beauties of paradise ("Author of 'The Rings': Tolkein's Catholic Journey," *Commonweal*, December 19, 2003).

The most popular fairy tales today, those of the brothers Grimm, are also profound religious tales from the pen of deeply religious men devoted to their Calvinistic Reformed faith tradition. To write these tales they drew on accounts ranging from ancient Egypt and Greece to medieval France. Wilhelm Grimm, in fact, was quite a mystic as well as an ecumenist who saw much value in pagan religions in so far as they reflected the Christian faith. He took the pagan tales and "baptized" them: water crossings that symbolized baptism, Christ in the form of noble princes, and helpful doves that evoke the Holy Spirit. The story of Hansel and Gretal was reworked into a classical parable of the journey of the human soul from infancy to spiritual awareness, of right and wrong, of human salvation.

In *Little Red Riding Hood* the three giant oak trees visible from Grandmother's house bind into one, an image of the Christian Trinity. Cinderella delves into the idea of the communion of saints where the heroine, her deceased mother, and the doves unite in love and charity. Snow White comes back to life through the agency of a prince, Christ in camouflage. (Radical feminists of a secular mindset, totally ignorant of the tale's religious core, have had Snow White banned in the public schools on the basis that it emphasizes a woman's dependence on a man for her life.

Sleeping Beauty (also banned in schools for the same reason) contains the themes of hell and the resurrection as the Christ-Prince breaks through the thorn barrier that surrounds the enchanted castle (death), and gives life through love.

Speaking of radical feminists provokes a comment on an area that deserves to be more fully treated, namely, the fluidity of story. With its interplay of teller and listener, this fluidity has been somewhat constricted up to now because stories have always been told and listened to, as narrated and interpreted, from a male point of view. This has provided some great insights but also very limited ones. Now a feminist reading of the biblical stories has expanded the potential of the story and will continue to enrich and challenge us in the future. For example, feminists remind us that important women in the Bible have long been overlooked.

Images point

Now back to a familiar point: if we would approach the Bible as a story book of oral tales told for the purposes of identity, support, and ethical guidance, and replete with symbolism, deeper meaning, and metaphors (some of which we have yet to understand), then some of the difficulties we have with this ancient book might disappear. And that brings us to an ever recurring warning that must be given over and over again: beware of getting stuck on the images.

Beware of embracing the literal. This is the besetting sin of the fundamentalists. (As a first step, of course, we must embrace the literal, take a look at the text itself—but not stop there. We must look behind the literal.) If the Bible said thunder and lightning, then thunder and lightning it was. If the Bible said it was night, then night it was. But stories, like all forms of art, are not to be seen; they are to be *seen through*. They offer not sight, but insight. They use imaginative language, creative images, camera angles, erratic brush strokes, background music, and things that are logically out of place or objectively pure invention to lead us to something else that lies behind. It's like the curator in a museum

who overheard two ladies stage-whispering their negative comments about some masterpieces. Finally, he could stand it no
longer. He went over and said to them, "Ladies, you are not here
to judge the paintings. They are here to judge you!"

The imagery is there to pull you into the painting and challenge something in you. The artist is saying something even if at
first you don't comprehend his or her "style" or the subject matter. Likewise, the evangelists are scribal artists. They make Jesus a
member of royalty, have angels come and minister to him, trans-
figure him on a mountain (like a Moses), have Moses and Elijah
(representing the Law and the Prophets) appear to him and the
wind and seas obey him because behind the language stands a
vindicated Risen One who is hard to describe but who had the
ability to give "living water."

I ask you keep in mind that, ideally, even the written Scripture
is a story in print and is meant to be publicly performed rather
than simply read. Since less than two percent of the ancients
could read, the few who could would not just read aloud to the
illiterate, but perform the reading. Performance, in its positive
not negative sense, should be the inspiration of all lectors. If it
were, then you and millions of other Catholics wouldn't be
hunched over missalettes reading along with the lector.

Can you imagine a Royal Shakespeare production of *King Lear*
with the audience hunched over their Folger texts, or a thousand
page-turners following the production of Arthur Miller's *Death of
a Salesman*? Yet that's what happens all over the country every
weekend in most Catholic parishes. Once more, the fixed print
has conquered the living oral word. We must liberate it.

13.

CENTRAL CASTING

There were a lot of scriptural storybooks around in the time of the Bible. Only seventy-two made it into the anthology. The Old Testament (forty-five books in all), received its final official canon around the second or third century BC, and the New Testament (twenty-seven books) received its final official canon around the third or fourth century AD.

As we saw in a previous chapter, there were a good number of gospels around at the same time, such as the Gospel of James, which came to be called the apocryphal gospels. So how did our four plus the other New Testament writings become part of the official canon? The bottom line is that we really don't know all the reasons why these twenty-seven books made it and others didn't, but we can hazard some guesses.

Most of the books were thought to have been written by one of Jesus' twelve apostles such as the letters of Peter, Paul, James, John (plus his book of Revelation), and Jude, even if church authorities discovered later that some of them could not have been written by those apostles. But they were now in the canon and so they remained. Then, those books held by the influential churches—the big power centers, so to speak—were accepted. Places like the church at Ephesus, Rome, Antioch, and so on. had influence just as New York or Chicago or Los Angeles influences the whole United States today. Finally, the books, no matter who actually wrote them, had to conform to the rule of faith.

Getting back to the gospels, at first there was no inclination at all to write a gospel. Why should there be? Jesus never wrote anything as far as we know nor did he command his disciples to do so. So Jesus' teachings were passed around orally. Then, too, everyone thought Jesus was coming back again, and very soon. This notion is found throughout the gospels and in Paul's epistles. It's no accident that the very last word of the last book of the New Testament is *Maranatha*, meaning "Come, Lord Jesus!" Since nobody was going to be around to read them, why write down the stories?

Paul's spotty letters were passed around but they were only letters and had no sense of permanency at the time. But by mid-60 AD two things happened. One, it became evident that Jesus had not returned; two, the apostles and first witnesses to the resurrection were dying off and there was a real danger that the Jesus story would be lost. So a "we're in it for the long haul" mentality began to kick in as seen in the later epistles attributed to Paul and other apostles, which began to take on a more universal and permanent character.

Lights, Camera, Action!

So now the stage is set for writing the permanent record. And the word "stage" conveniently returns us to our movie metaphor of the last chapter. Here, let's go to central casting. When a movie is on the drawing board, a group of consultants is called in to suggest who might play the leading roles. Tom Cruise, for example, will be chosen to play the romantic lead and not Don Knotts. In other words, the movie's plot, the tone of the movie, the genre (science fiction or comedy), the social context of the time, and the overall intent of the film will determine how to portray the main, pivotal character. The social context means that the conditions prevalent in society at the time the movie is made—war, racism, pornography, political correctness, for example—will subtly influence the movie's shape. Then it's up to the director to assemble all the parts and, with his casting material at hand, weave everything into the final product.

The director is key. The really great ones all leave their signature mark so you have no doubt whose work it is. I saw a movie capsule once which gave this description: "The quintessential western, the John Ford way." No question about it: you can spot the work of this genius a mile away. He has a distinctive approach to the story, the scenery, the camera angles. Alfred Hitchcock, Fred Zinneman, George Cukor, Preston Sturges, Steven Spielberg, Frank Capra, William Wyler, and Elia Kazin, all leave their mark. No one of them will tell the same cinematic story the same way. Neither did those "directors" we call the evangelists. Let's take a look at them.

Around the late 60s or early 70s AD, someone whom we later called Mark wrote the first gospel. It was produced in hindsight and naturally colored by his social context: the Christian experience of the decades since Jesus, also and importantly, the current problems a young Christianity was facing. Consensus is that Mark wrote his gospel in Rome and it was intended for the Gentile converts who were ignorant of Judaism. This is why Mark takes time to explain Jewish customs, which he wouldn't have to do if his audience were Jews.

I must say that Director Mark's final production (the gospel) is not a happy one. It's a kind of film noir, filled with sorrow and pain. He is obviously reflecting the contemporary suffering of the Roman Christians during the persecution of the emperor Nero during which some went bravely to their deaths, while others apostatized. And, it was rumored, some even squealed on the others; that's how Peter and Paul got caught up in the Roman net and were sent to their deaths. In any case, morale was low. Thus, by focusing so intently on the suffering and death of Jesus, Mark is telling his compatriots that suffering is part and parcel of Christianity because the moral, holy life will always rub evildoers the wrong way and they will retaliate. Mark's "movie" reflects the cry of the psalmist:

> Do not be silent, O God of my praise.
> For wicked and deceitful mouths are opened against me,
>   speaking against me with lying tongues.
> They beset me with words of hate,
>   and attack me without cause.
> In return for my love they accuse me,
>   even while I make prayer for them. (Psalm 109:1–4)

Mark is saying that seriously following Jesus is always something of a martyrdom. But hang in there: all will be made new again. Also, of all the evangelists, in trying to counter statements that Jesus was not truly human but only a divine being pretending to be so, Mark gives us a very human Jesus, full of emotions, anguish, and passion. The closest modern film to Mark is the Italian director's Paolo Pasolini's film, *The Gospel According to Saint Matthew*.

A Time-warp Jesus

Before we proceed to the next evangelist-director, we must take time out here to repeat a point we made in previous chapters, namely, that the evangelists (the original writers, adapters, and redactors of the gospel) consistently "upgraded" Jesus. That is, they were not interested in preserving Jesus' exact words, reflecting his own particular time and place, but of preserving his teaching and adapting his words for *this* time and *this* place so that others might believe. Simply put, they co-opted Jesus in responding to their immediate needs and pressures. A good ready-made example is the way the gospels treat the Pharisees, whose very name connotes to us hypocrisy, deceit, and rigid bureaucracy. Actually, the Pharisees were a pretty good bunch, and there is some scholarly speculation that Jesus himself was one.

But in Jesus' time the Pharisees were minor players. There were very few of them and they were not politically influential, so they hardly warranted the diatribes that Mark and Matthew put into Jesus' mouth. So, what's going on here? What is going on is that, by the time of the evangelists, the Pharisees had, in fact, become quite important in Jewish life—especially after the destruction of the Temple by the Romans in the year 70 put their powerful rivals, the Sadducees and priests, out of a job. In fact, the Romans wound up letting the Pharisees run civil affairs, and so it was that they often came into conflict with the Jewish Christians and gave them a hard time.

Remember, in John's gospel it is recorded that the Pharisees threw the followers of Jesus out of the synagogue. Remember, too, the famous Pharisee whose life's mission was to persecute the Christians: his name was Paul. So what you have in the gospels is not Jesus of Nazareth blasting the minority-party Pharisees in the year 30, but Jesus adapted to blasting the majority-party Pharisees of the year 70 or 90. If this upsets you, try to remember the rules of story. In true storytelling form, Jesus' insistence on interior motivation, purity, and love—true religion was not merely a question of externals—is a genuine exposition of his teaching, the real core tradition going back to him. The latter day application of the gospel times are creative details that expand the core but do not depart from it.

With that in mind, we fast forward to ten or twenty years after Mark's production, to the gospels of Matthew and Luke. They both copied a lot of Mark, but then too, a lot had happened since his time so they upgraded him, explained him, and improved on him. They also added story material gathered elsewhere that Mark apparently knew nothing about.

First, let's look at Matthew—remembering that he, like all the others, is a composite figure; therefore, there are layers of texts from different people and times patched together to form the final edition of this gospel. He wrote in Antioch in Syria around the mid 80s. Antioch was the third largest city in the Greco-

Roman empire and had a large Jewish population. Keeping in mind his audience, he frames his gospel around Jesus as the new Moses, a device that will resonate well with the Jews.

Remember that all four productions are propaganda pieces in the best sense. Therefore, Matthew casts Jesus as Moses, the great lawgiver, and frames his "movie" around a group of pronouncements or teachings, the most famous of which is the collection we know as the Sermon on the Mount. If Jesus is a "new Moses," then like Moses he must teach from the mountaintop, and so Matthew pans his camera there. (Recall that Luke, the social justice advocate, must have Jesus preach that sermon from the plain, among the simple folk.)

Moreover, since the Jews of Antioch were devoted to the five books of the Torah, Matthew constructed his book around five books of sermons or discourses. The idea was that he was replacing the five scrolls of the Pentateuch with Jesus. Again, like Mark, Matthew also pushes Jesus' times into his times. For example, he has Jesus warn, "Beware of them, for they will hand you over to councils and flog you in their synagogues; and you will be dragged before governors and kings because of me, as a testimony to them and the Gentiles" (10:17–18). Well, that's precisely what was happening in Matthew's time, not Jesus'. You catch the hint when he has Jesus say they will expel you from their synagogues; the Christians had already been expelled. The seven parables Matthew records are likewise meant to be applicable to the young church. That's why he also changes Jesus' stories to fit his own time. The parable of the widely scattered seed, for example, (13:18–23) was likely first meant by Jesus to show the Father's extraordinary generosity but Matthew turns into into an allegory of the trials that a life of faith can bring.

Likewise, Matthew's production, now aware that Jesus was evidently not returning very soon (consequently, Matthew advises us to lead a life of vigilance, for only the Father knows when Jesus is coming back and he's not telling [24:36]), begins to lay organizational groundwork for the long haul. Matthew is further con-

cerned about the quality of this now-to-endure Christian community. Thus he warns about the use and misuse of power
("whoever becomes like a child is greatest in the kingdom of
heaven"), directs that it must be a reconciling community ("forgive seven times seven") that must avoid scandal and solve its
own internal problems (don't be taking each other to the civil
courts), and be guided by a life of prayer ("where two or three are
gathered, there I am"); and finally, he reminds them that all will
be ultimately judged anyway on how they have treated their
brothers and sisters ("when I was hungry, you gave me"—or did
not—"to eat," and so on, chapter 25). You can see that Matthew's
gospel is a very different kind of production from Mark's.

Luke and John

Then there is Luke. He was a Gentile Christian also writing somewhere outside of Palestine. (Come to think of it, all the books of
the New Testament—with the possible exception of the epistle of
Peter—were written outside of Palestine, a fact that underscores
all the adapting that went on.) Luke is a sensitive "director." He
has a special resonance with the poor, which might suggest that
he lived among the affluent and was reminding them of their
obligation to the less fortunate.

Luke's gospel has several unique themes. As we have noted
elsewhere, he soft-pedals the faults of the apostles, and gives
women a prominent place in his gospel (although, for all of that,
he never presents a woman as holding any official position or
office). His gospel has the largest collection of parables including
the famous ones of the Good Samaritan and the Prodigal Son.
Luke is fond of table fellowship and gives us poignant scenes of
the exchanges that go on there. In his gospel he stresses prayer
and underscores mercy and forgiveness. His second volume, the
Acts of the Apostles, refers a great deal to the workings of the
Holy Spirit and the need for unity and apostolic authority.

John is another story altogether. He is far different from the
first three evangelists, who have much in common. He is not the

apostle John but likely one of John's followers who wrote around the year 90 or 100. His account shows signs of later editing and additions so, like all the books of the Bible, a lot of people had a hand in the final production.

John's book was written for a community that was going through its own particular problems on the brink of the second century. For one thing, as we mentioned above, the Christians here were being tossed out of the local synagogues by the Pharisees so there is a great deal of animosity towards them. John and the other evangelists refer to them somewhat disparagingly as "the Jews," even though only a certain class, the leaders and *not* the general populace, were involved in acts against Jesus. The nasty words put into Jesus' mouth—for example, "You are from your father the devil" (Jn 8:44)—reflect this hostility. In other words, the phrase "the Jews" used negatively in Matthew, Mark, and Luke reflects a family rift, a nasty divorce between the traditional Jews and those who followed Jesus.

By the time of John's gospel the label "Jews" became a code word for all who opposed their fellow Jew, Jesus, with murderous intent; they were all regarded as hostile authorities. Though it may seem like anti-Semitism, it is not, but rather, a type of family infighting, which often can be far more vicious. It's Jews railing against Jews. It's something like white supremists killing white civil rights workers. Neither are anti-American, but both are Americans killing each other in the name of what they think is right. Unfortunately, subsequent Christians, especially when they separated from the synagogue, forgot that this was a family feud and turned it into an "us against them" scenario. The Jewish Babylonian Talmud cursed anyone who went over to Christ (a Jew), while the Christian writings of the Church Fathers called the Jews "God-killers." And it all went downhill from there, into racism and mutual persecution.

Getting back to John, he is, as we said, different. His language, his style, his use of symbols such as light and darkness, flesh and spirit, and figures of speech and irony—he's fond of double meanings—all single out John. There are no parables of Jesus in his book, only those very long discourses that go on and on, and there is virtually no mention of the kingdom of God, which figured so prominently in the other gospels. John makes Jesus into a kind of divine figure walking a few feet above the ground, who constantly speaks about himself with "I am" sayings: "I am..." the bread of life, the light of the world, the gate for the sheep, the good shepherd, the resurrection and the life, the way, truth, and life, the true vine. That "I am," of course, resonates with the Old Testament revelation to Moses. In short, Jesus is God and indeed God among us (the incarnation), who performs not miracles but "signs," that point to himself.

Some of John's symbols are disguised: the wedding feast at Cana is not a wedding feast at all but a sign that a new era is here with an abundance of wine and food; the healing of the Gentile servant and the conversion of his whole household says that Jesus came for all; the feeding of the five thousand reveals that Jesus is the fulfillment of the Exodus; his walking on the water is Jesus conquering chaos, those chaotic waters at the beginning of creation; Lazarus' raising, coming as it does as Jesus is on the way to his own death, foretells his own resurrection; and the washing of the feet tells us how we should celebrate the Eucharist, that is, by living it. Jesus' farewell discourses imitate those of other great biblical leaders such as Moses and Joshua, using figures of choseness such as the vine and branches, and offering words of comfort. John would be equivalent to the great Swedish director, Ingmar Bergman.

A Reminder

We must backtrack a bit and remind you that the gospels were written solely for the early Christian community. That may sound odd to us who think otherwise, but the fact is the gospels were never meant for outside readers. They were never intended for *all* peoples in *all* times but simply to hold the first-century Christians loyal to the experience of God in Jesus.

The evangelists never envisaged that Western strangers of another century would be interested in their work, much less studying it. They wrote for the occasion; that is, as we have seen, for the needs of this particular group, this third generation group of Christians who wanted to know about the first generation experience. That's why, as we have noted, the gospels "rework" Jesus for this audience. They were meant to bind them together, to give them comfort, affirmation and a sense of commonality reminding them that they were spiritual kin, brothers and sisters. The gospel writers could care less about outsiders, present or future, and were not out to convert anybody. If an outsider got hold of one of the gospels and was in fact converted, that was strictly a happy accident.

It should be quite apparent now that the gospels were in no way intended to be biographies of Jesus. There are obviously too many gaps: the accounts of his childhood and his youth are sketchy at best; information about his adopted father, Joseph, his grandparents, and other relatives, his education, work, and so on, are all missing. (Remember, this is what drove the pious folk crazy and so they invented the apocryphal gospels to fill in the gaps.) The evangelists had something other than biography in mind: sharing and preserving the good news stories of Jesus, the *evangelium*, which is accurately translated as "good news spoken to a live audience who believed in him already."

Different stories travelled to different parts of the Mediterranean and were collected by people (the evangelists) of that region. Perhaps one might profitably think of the gospels as portraits rather than biographies.

14.

THE BIBLE AS MIRROR AND VIEWPOINT

Since the Bible is a storybook, it contains stories about people. That seems commonsensical enough to say, but we take this truth for granted. The Bible is basically all about people and their relationship to God. And since the right relationship with God is its central motif, the Bible's emphasis is on what these people say and do that help or hurt that relationship. This explains—and here you have to stop and think about it—why there are no descriptions of people in the Bible, descriptions that we moderns automatically expect and yearn for.

Again, think about it: almost never are there descriptions in the Scripture stories. What did the biblical people look like? Were they handsome and beautiful, homely and ugly? How tall or short were they? Where did they live, what did they eat, and what did they wear? What were their hobbies? These are items we media-conditioned moderns think are absolutely necessary to the story. Look at how our hunger for this information about our celebrities keeps whole industries of fan magazines, paparazzi, and TV biography shows working around the clock to satisfy. Our movie-conscious age simply must have images, and so we make Moses look like Charlton Heston, Judas like Johnny Depp, David like Tom Cruise, Esther like Ava Gardner, Judith like Meryl Streep, Zacchaeus like Danny DeVito, Paul like Russell Crowe, and Rahab like Goldie Hawn.

But that's *our* age, *our* conceits, not the Bible's. Outside of a rare exception—such as Saul being tall or Absalom having long hair or Zacchaeus being short because these attributes were critical to their stories—there are no descriptions of anyone in the Bible, and that includes Jesus. There's not even any real description or setting the stage of scenes in the Bible. These things didn't matter to the ancients. Again, the emphasis is on people: men, women, kings, prophets, disciples, fools, magicians, warriors, slaves, and fishermen, and how they all related to God. Fortunately for us, however, these description-less people talk a lot, and their spoken words fill most of the books of the Bible (there's that oral foundation again). Those words, those conversations, always raise, in one way or another, the critical question that defines the Bible: are the biblical people listening to God or not?

Since we know by what ensues in the biblical stories that the people were indeed listening to God, the next implied question for the reader is this: are we they? Are we two-faced Jacob, conniving Rebecca, homely Leah, Job filled with fury and doubt at the unfairness of life? Are we Noah who walked with God, Caleb who believed in God's promise when others wavered, pharaoh of the hard heart, Hannah who prayed for the gift of life, Ruth the foreigner who remained loyal to God's people? Are we Saul who sought people's approval more than God's, David who both loved and sinned, Solomon the wise man who was a fool, Zechariah who was so perplexed, Joseph who, in spite of rumors, remained loyal? Are we Mary Magdalene who was the first to announce the Good News of the resurrection, Thomas who doubted, Peter who wavered, Pilate who compromised Jesus to death, Nicodemus who sought, Simon who helped carry a cross, the sidelined women of Jerusalem who could do nothing but weep, the adulteress to whom mercy was shown? Are we Dorcas who was full of good works, Barnabas who encouraged, Simeon who tried to buy spiritual gifts? The list could go on and on. The point is, there is a component of identity and challenge in the stories of the Bible. There are no descriptions of biblical folk in those stories because they are we: we are the description.

The Bible is a mirror. Looking into it brings bad news before it brings good news. It is the news that we are sinners, but it is also the news that God loves us anyway. That is the spiritual focus we must bring to the biblical stories if their message is to come alive for us, here and now.

Strange Saints

In the litany of people we just mentioned, we might notice that the biblical notion of hero and heroine—saints, we might call them—differs from ours. In our culture, we celebrate the celebrity no matter how shameless or exploitative he or she may be. Our heroes emanate from power, fame, money, and sex. Our adulation is evident in the astronomical amounts of money we pay them. The biblical heroes, on the other hand, while fairly shameless and duplicitous (one thinks of Jacob, David, or Peter), emanate from their relationship with God. For the biblical writers, a saint wasn't one who necessarily led a virtuous life but one who, however unvirtuous, was suddenly called by God and responded, perhaps even to their own surprise.

Take one heroine of Scripture, Rahab, a scarlet prostitute. Why is she a heroine? Because of her faith in the God who called and to whom she found herself responding. Let me jog your memory about this Old Testament story. Joshua, Moses' successor, has led the army of Israel to the threshold of the promised land. Then spies are sent to reconnoiter Jericho. As soldiers often do, they end up at Rahab's place in a seedy section of town.

Somehow, the king got word that spies were about the city, and so he sent the police to seize them. When they inquired at Rahab's house, she lied. Batting her heavy eyelashes she said, "True, a couple of Hebrew boys were here earlier, but when the gate was closed at dark, they left; go quickly and maybe you'll overtake them." The king's men rushed on, not knowing that Madame Rahab had hidden the Israelites on her roof. Had they been found, it would have cost her her life. She knew that but she did it anyway. Why? Because, as she told the spies, she had heard of the mighty works of their God, and all she asked in return was that the Israelites show her family mercy when the walls of Jericho came tumbling down.

Later that night, Rahab lets the spies down by a rope, tying a scarlet thread in her window to identify her place for the invading Israelites. When Joshua and his army finally enter the city, those in the red thread house in the red light district were the only ones spared as the invaders leveled Jericho. Thus Rahab, who put her life on the line for Yahweh, became a celebrated heroine. (See Josh 2:1—6:27 for the full account.)

A prostitute. A liar. What kind of a saint is that? What's worse, she's not alone. Drunk and naked Noah, Abraham and his squabbling family, mean-spirited, conniving old Sarah, murderer Moses, lustful David, bigoted Paul—all unholy as we would label them. Yet the Bible honors them as saints. If that puzzles you—and it should—you should know once again that the Bible simply has a different notion of sainthood than we do.

A biblical saint is not a person who lives a virtuously throughout his or her life. No, biblical saintliness is a matter of what God does with people and how they respond. A person is called a saint in the Bible because God wants that person to do something holy, *not* because that person *is* holy. Biblical saints are those called to do God's work and accept, no matter how unworthy or shady they are. Sainthood in the Bible is being commandeered by God no matter how wicked you are, and doing what God wants. In short, biblical saints are those who listen to God and, at least this one critical time, say "yes" regardless of the mess they are and the risk they have to take. It's their moment of grace as it were, and they take it. And all is redeemed.

In the Bible, an evil person can claim sainthood by accepting a noble deed regardless of the cost. Contemporary candidates would be Oskar Schindler, who, by all accounts, was a despicable man. Yet he risked his life to save countless Jews during the Holocaust. In Dickens' *Tale of Two Cities*, Sidney Carton, who was quite self-centered, took another's place at the guillotine. To wax homiletic, what the Bible is saying is that for all of us, there is or will be, a golden moment of heroism. It need not be large or dramatic or mighty or earth-shattering. It can be something as quiet as taking the blame for someone else and living with disgrace, or keeping a secret that would destroy another's career—things we might ordinarily do gladly and gleefully.

But this one time, God calls us to do the noble thing and for some reason, maybe one not even clear to ourselves, we say "yes." It could be that in a lifetime of selfishness we are presented with the opportunity to perform a totally selfless act of love and generosity and, uncharacteristically, we grasp it. (One thinks of the Good Thief.) For once in our life, as the saying goes, we do something profoundly decent. And in that moment all our sins are forgotten. No matter what our history, how bad a person we have been, how tepid and indifferent a Christian, we will have become a biblical saint for charity covers a multitude of sins.

The Viewpoint

If the biblical people reflect our lives and their stories beg our identification, they also beg our openness to the flexibility of those stories, a point we made in the opening chapters of this book. Many biblical stories are open to several interpretations depending on where you're coming from. Norton Juster's wonderful book for children (and adults), *The Phantom Tollbooth*, makes this point. In the story, the boy, Milo, travels to the Kingdom of Knowledge. Everywhere he goes, Milo learns life lessons. Here is a lesson from a character named Alec Bings at the "Point of View" Station:

> "From here that looks like a bucket of water," Alec said, pointing to a bucket of water. "But from an ant's point of view, it's a vast ocean, from an elephant's, just a cool drink, and to a fish, of course, it's home. So, you see, the way you see things depends a great deal on where you look at them from."

It's no different with Scripture. We've already seen that people in the Mediterranean world saw things differently than we do, and how hard we have to work not to impose our values on the people and times of the Bible. So let's take some examples of a different point of view. Here's a familiar story from the gospels:

> Jesus entered Jericho and was passing through it. A man was there named Zacchaeus; he was a chief tax collector and was rich. He was trying to see who Jesus was, but on account of the crowd he could not, because he was short in stature. So he ran ahead and climbed a sycamore tree to see him, because he was going to pass that way. When Jesus came to the place, he looked up and said to him, "Zacchaeus, hurry and come down; for I must stay at your house today." So he hurried down and was happy to welcome him. All who saw it began to grumble and said, "He has gone to be the guest of one who is a sinner." Zacchaeus stood there and said to the Lord, "Look, half of my possessions, Lord, I will give to the poor; and if I have defrauded anyone of anything, I will pay back four times as much." Then Jesus said to him, "Today salvation has come to this house, because he too is a son of Abraham. For the Son of Man came to seek out and to save the lost." (Lk 19:1–10)

We've heard this gospel dozens of times at Mass, and the preacher properly expounds the well-worn theme of conversion. We are urged to be like Zacchaeus, renounce our sinful self, and, a new person, fall at the feet of Jesus where we will meet mercy and forgiveness.

But there's another point of view about this episode that lifts it out of a conversion motif to a Mediterranean honor-shame motif, which may, in fact, be closer to the truth. Look at it this way. Zacchaeus and the crowd have two opposing views. To the crowd Zacchaeus, being a wealthy tax collector, is a greedy bum. In the Mediterranean world of poverty and limited resources, there were only so many resources to go around, only one nine-inch pie if you will. If you have too much, too large a piece, that automatically means someone else has less, a smaller piece. Therefore, being rich means being greedy means being indifferent to others.

Now, Zacchaeus was not so much a tax collector as a regional director who oversaw the tax collectors. The Romans would levy a certain amount of tax on a municipality, which the tax collector paid out of his own pocket in a lump sum. It was then up to him to recoup what he had paid plus whatever additional money he could squeeze out of the people: that was his profit. It was a chancy game. Sometimes he lost (you can't squeeze blood out of a stone), but sometimes he struck it rich.

Anyway, because of his job, the crowd automatically saw Zacchaeus as evil, wicked. He was prejudged. But was their estimation accurate? Further, was that the way Zacchaeus saw himself? There is evidence that he did not. He may have seen himself as a righteous man who was badly misunderstood. What did he say? "Look, half of my possessions, Lord, I will give to the poor; and if I have defrauded anyone of anything, I will pay back four times as much." He doesn't say, "I *will* give half my belongings to charity," but, as the Greek construction of his words indicate, he says "I *customarily* do that. That's the kind of a guy I am. I do this as a matter of pious routine. It's a part of my life. And, what's more, if it so happened that I did in fact cheat someone, I'll make a fourfold return—a recompense far beyond what rabbinical or Roman law demands."

Jesus is delighted with Zacchaeus' response and must have looked around as if to say, "See how you misjudged this man, this son of Abraham? Aren't you ashamed?" To cap his approval, Jesus says, "Today, salvation has come to this house." You must remember that Jesus, or Yeshua, means salvation in Hebrew. In other words, Jesus is saying, "Hey, this is a man after my own heart. I'm going into his house and have a brew with him."

Seeing this story from another point of view—a more accurate one, according to scholars—we have, not an account of a conversion, but an account of rash judgment, of prejudice, of how others see us and how we see ourselves. People who have been misjudged, misunderstood, unappreciated, or the object of nasty rumors have a friend in this parable-story.

The Drive-you-crazy Stories

Then there are the Bible stories that drive you up the wall or make you shudder. In the book of Numbers, for instance, Yahweh announces the "ethnic cleansing" of Canaan. As a matter of fact, in no way does Yahweh appear to be angry with the Canaanites. Unlike the Egyptians, the Canaanites are never presented as guilty of any offense against Israel. They are just in the way of its expansion, and because of this they may pose a threat to Israel's religion. Their only offense, it seems, is that they worship their own gods and live on land for which the Lord has other plans. No matter. They are doomed. They will not be offered the option of conversion or given the offer of coexisting with Israel and maintaining their own ways. Yahweh's unilateral decision is to exterminate them. And so Moses tells the Israelites about to invade Canaan to enslave the people if they surrender and kill all the males if they don't take the women as booty, and to not let a soul remain alive. That's pretty scary.

Remember also the incident in which Yahweh slays all the scouts but two when they bring back news from Canaan (Num 11) and disallows Moses to enter Canaan. When a fresh rebellion breaks out against Moses and Aaron, the Lord punishes the rebels by having the earth swallow them alive (Num 16:30). The next day the Lord slays 14,700 of them. He visits the iniquity of parent upon children and children's children to the third and fourth generation, and grim is Israel's fate if they do not observe God's law.

Here's more bloodletting: the book of Judges is a collection of stories of guerrilla bands. A story that runs through Judges 19:1— 21:25 even pits the Israelites against one another over the horrible gang rape and murder of a concubine, whose owner then cuts her into twelve pieces and sends the body parts to the tribes of Israel. Eleven of the tribes then rise up against the tribe of Benjamin, killing all the men, women, children, and livestock and burning down their town. Only a few escape. Belatedly realizing that the tribe might then die out altogether, they seize a forgotten Benjaminite town, killing all the inhabitants but saving the virgin girls, giving them over to be raped by the few male survivors. Stephen King could do no better.

Who wants to read stuff like this? It's not bedside reading or stories you tell to the children. Stories like these have always unnerved people and embarrassed scholars,who have a hard time explaining away such violence.

But, remember, not only is this storytelling but primitive storytelling, and the primitive mind told stories that would impress other primitive minds. God really didn't say or do all those terrible things. But in the hyperbole of storytelling, he had to: there were points to be made. One critical one was that God is sovereign; God is the Lord of all; God is the author of life; God both gives and takes away. God is in charge; no one judges God.

Job learned this lesson the hard way. Just as Job is complaining that life isn't fair (how often have we expressed that truism!), and his friends are trying to hold onto the old covenant theology that good is always rewarded and evil always punished, God appears, furious that Job has questioned him. God asserts his power to create ("Where were you when I laid the foundations of the earth?"), letting it be known that Job, or anyone else for that matter, exists solely due to his power. God is power, has power, and it is not to be questioned. You simply obey, for without God nothing exists.

We must all learn this basic fact. People must learn to fear and respect God. It's always God's call. The canticle found in 1 Samuel 2:2-7 says it all:

> My heart exults in the Lord; my strength is exalted in my God. My mouth derides my enemies, because I rejoice in my victory. There is no Holy One like the Lord, no one besides you; there is no Rock like our God....The Lord kills and brings to life; he brings down to Sheol and raises up. The Lord makes poor and makes rich; he brings low, he also exalts....The Lord! His adversaries shall be shattered; the Most High will thunder in heaven. The Lord will judge the ends of the earth; he will give strength to his king, and exalt the power of his anointed.

In the New Testament, Paul, a Mediterranean man, tries his hand at explaining:

> What then are we to say? Is there injustice on God's part? By no means! For he says to Moses, "I will have mercy on whom I have mercy, and I will have compassion on whom I have compassion." So it depends not on human will or exertion, but on God who shows mercy. For the scripture says to Pharaoh, "I have raised you up for the very purpose of showing my power in you, so that my name may be proclaimed in all the earth." So then he has mercy on whomever he chooses, and he hardens the heart of whomever he chooses (Rom 9:14–18).

"So there!" is the understood peroration.

There's a logic here that escapes us moderns but works quite well for the ancients. To understand it we have to step into their shoes. The biblical writers so embraced the fundamental conviction that God indeed was intractably sovereign and omnipotent over the entire world that they were quite able to see him as the author of good and evil. Thus Isaiah has God say, "I form light and create darkness, I make weal and create woe" (45:7).

The sacred writers were so obsessed with loudly confessing God's unlimited power that they easily let slip by the issues of his fairness and virtue—matters that concern us but not them. That's why they can blithely write that God hardened Pharaoh's heart, "incited" David to take a census and then punished him for taking it (although the author of Chronicles cleans up the story and says that Satan incited the taking of the census), and caused the prophets to speak lies in order to lure a king to his death (1 Kings 22). That's why, in view of the necessity of Israel's survival in order to produce the Messiah, Yahweh had every right to annihilate the Amalekites, who were bent on destroying Israel.

God is Lord of all. And so from their point of view, the Old Testament authors had to construct stories that were not literally true but true as "propaganda," symbolically true. They had a point to make, and in their time, that was the only way they knew to make it. It may not have been our way, but we are not them and they are not us.

Labor-Management

Let's turn to something more palatable, if no less irritating: the parable of the early and latecomer workers who all receive the same pay (Mt 20:1–16). Work twelve hours, get fifty bucks. Work one hour, get fifty bucks. 'T ain't fair. The best way I can handle this story is to share a homily I gave on it. Like Alec Bings in *The Phantom Tollbooth*, I present a different point of view:

> Each year we have this parable. Each year we find it irritating. Each year we amusedly listen to the preacher try to square the circle, try to make an unfair situation sound fair. Imagine, giving someone who works only one hour the same pay as someone who worked twelve hours! It doesn't wash. But it's not as nonsensical as it sounds if you take the parable out of our modern context and put it in the biblical context, with all the other crazy parables that are giving the same incredible message; that, with unsettling exaggeration, slap us in the face with delightful surprises. Let me review

four of them that are precise variations on our gospel today, and you'll begin to see the point.

First, there is the parable of the unforgiving servant with its message of God's extraordinary capacity to forgive someone with a huge debt he couldn't possibly pay back. Then there are the more familiar stories of the lost sheep, the story of the lost coin, and the story of the prodigal son. You know them well. In each of these stories we see how almighty God acts towards us in a way which we would not naturally expect. They all reveal a God who comes to us in love and mercy not as a harsh judge who justifiably wants to punish us for our sins.

These five parables show God's radical and surprising ways with us. No first-century king, for example, would forgive a person's huge debt any more than Visa or Mastercard would cancel thousands of dollars of credit card debt. No sensible shepherd would leave ninety-nine sheep at huge risk to go looking for one measly lost animal. No sane woman would sweep her house for hours looking for a single lost coin worth ten cents. And certainly no first-century father would freely forgive his wayward son, running to meet him and then throwing a party to celebrate his return. A proper father would put the son on probation for a while to see if he was serious about repenting.

Likewise, in today's parable, the workers who had toiled all day in the oppressive heat complained. They felt they had been cheated when they discovered that those who started work only an hour before quitting time got the same pay as they did. But, you see, it's the same dynamic at work here as in the other parables: the late-hour workers in today's parable are the indebted servant, the lost sheep, the lost coin, and the prodigal son. They are all the same character.

In all these stories Jesus is claiming that each of us is of infinite worth to almighty God, no matter who we are or what we have done or not done, how long we have or haven't worked. All fringe, indebted, lost, latecomer folk are given undeserved kindness and mercy. Do you see the point? This is not a parable about fairness or labor-management relations. It's a story about God, who leaves ninety-nine to search for one, who sweeps a house for ten cents, who embraces a son who had fled him, and who gives one-hour laborers too much money. It's a story designed to take our breath away and ask, "what kind of a God is this who subverts all human expectations?"

One of my favorite plays is *Les Miserables*. It's a great story that played on Broadway for eighteen years, with fabulous music as many of you know. Based on the novel by Victor Hugo, the central character in the story is Jean Valjean. The play starts with Valjean being released after nineteen years in prison. He is a bitter man because he had been sentenced to jail for stealing a loaf of bread to feed the children in his family. Freed at last, Valjean is denied food and lodging in a village even though he has some money because no one wants an ex-convict around. Finally, a kindly bishop invites him home, offering him a meal and a bed. When Valjean dines with him, the bishop insists on putting his finest silver plates, used only for special guests, out on the table.

During the night Valjean wakes up, steals the bishop's silver plates, and sneaks out of the house. The police soon catch him. He lies about the silver plates, saying that the bishop gave them to him as a gift. The police take Valjean back to the bishop's house with the stolen goods. When Valjean returns to the bishop's house in police custody, the bishop exclaims that he is glad to see him because he wanted to give him the silver candlesticks as well. The gendarmes have no choice but to let him go. This amazing act of forgiveness and mercy makes such a deep impression on Jean Valjean that he is transformed into a new person and spends the rest of his life serving others and showing mercy to them.

Think: the bishop is the forgiving Master of the indebted

servant, the farmer pursuing the lost sheep, the house sweeper searching for a lousy dime, the father embracing his hippie son. He acts irrationally. Who puts out silverware for a bum? Who pretends that he gave away his silver to the same bum and is glad he's back to claim the candlesticks as well? Don't you see? The bishop is God; he is the Master in today's gospel who acts generously to people who did not earn or deserve his generosity.

Now do you catch the point of the parable? God acts in your life and in mine in this same way. God, thank heaven, shows us grace and mercy when we least deserve it and like Jean Valjean, we are transformed when we truly experience such gracious love. We are freed to serve others, diligently doing good works with no need to keep score any more.

If you want a summary of this gospel, here it is: there were the cries of the lost servant, the lost sheep, the lost coin, the lost son, and the lost workers. This parable says that, unbelievably, their cries were heard and God, who lost both his mind and his heart, went and found them.

End of homily. When you think about it, the first-come/late-come workers scenario really replays the theme of the horrors we saw in the books of Numbers and Judges: God is sovereign, the Master of his gifts. It's just that, in a different time and place, the stories play out differently. But stories they are and that's why we remember them.

15.

TOLD AND
SCRIPTED

At this point, it might be helpful as a summary to further illustrate how storytelling works in the Scriptures. In this chapter I will use examples from the New Testament simply because it's more familiar to the average reader than the Old Testament.

We first have to repeat that the gospels were not written by eyewitnesses. That is a common truism among scholars but, alas, a scandal to non-scholars who quickly point out that clearly, Matthew and John were apostles, so there! How could they not be eyewitnesses? Besides, their names are in the title. The answer is that, in fact, someone in the second century added the titles and the names. Nowhere in the gospels themselves—or in most of the remaining twenty books of the New Testament, for that matter—is the author mentioned. We speak freely of the epistles of John, Peter, James, and Jude but there is no identification in the books themselves that says these are the people who wrote them. More shock: even in those books that do carry the name of an author, someone else really wrote it using the name of an apostle. Paul, for example; even though his name is in those letters, he did not write the epistles to Timothy or Titus or Ephesians or Colossians or Hebrews.

What kind of chicanery is happening here, you ask? There is no chicanery, no deceit. We must simply remember that in ancient times it was quite conventional to attribute a work to a famous person. Everybody did it and no one was fooled (except later generations who forgot the convention). Yes, Moses was said to have written the first five books of the Bible (the Pentateuch) but he hardly could have done so since his death is recorded in book five (Deuteronomy). Isaiah did not write the entire book that bears his name (there are at least three authors involved) nor Daniel "his" book. Solomon, the wise man personified, is said to be the author of the wisdom book that bears his name and David, the lofty musician, is said to have written the 150 psalms, but in fact neither are the authors.

On the other hand, think of it this way: what names other than these would *you* use if you wanted to get your book read? What would get us slapped into jail for plagarism in our day would not be noticed in ancient times, because back then using a "celebrity" name to give weight and authority to a book was a common convention. That's the way it was and we have to judge such matters by their times, not ours.

Getting back to the gospel authors, they simply could not have been Matthew, Mark, Luke, and John; internal evidence precludes that. For example, why would Matthew copy so substantially from Mark's gospel if he were an apostle, therefore, an eyewitness, and Mark was not? It doesn't make sense. No, the names of the gospel authors were educated guesses made by Christians of the second century. Note further that those gospel authors, not being eyewitnesses, were second generation Christians, inheritors of the oral tradition. As inheritors they had a lot of stories, which, if you will permit some fancy, they jotted down on index cards. So when it came time to compile the oral tradition—gather the index cards into a paper, if you will—they had to make choices.

Since the writers were not actually there, how would they arrange the material on the index cards? They wound up doing what you and I would do: they determined their main plot or overall theme, determined the audience for whom they were writing (their target audience, to use a marketing term), and particularly considered the current problems they had to face. They realized they had to "update" Jesus in order to effectively respond to their audience, and they proceeded very much like the movie directors I used as an example in a previous chapter. Consequently, they left us, not a strict biography, since that was not their intention, but rather, an interpretation of the life, words, and deeds of someone who had both changed and challenged their world. (Like the little boy, remember, who described his lost mother as the most beautiful lady in the world.)

There are, of course, biographical details, but they are subverted to the overall intent. And since the evangelists were writing for their own generation, the Jesus story, as I said above, is placed in that context. Why not? The people of that era wanted to know how to live according to the teaching of Jesus in their own time and place, and so they often lifted Jesus out of his context and put him into theirs. This explains why we have four different gospels with four different viewpoints dictated by the needs of the audience. This also explains why the material is arranged differently in each of the accounts.

In one famous example, Matthew takes his index card with the story of Jesus driving the money changers in the Temple and sticks it at the end of his gospel (chapter 21) because it fits in better there as a climax leading up to the crucifixion. John has a different agenda. He wants to show Jesus' authority and divinity right from the start so he flips his card to the front of his gospel (chapter 2). In true storytelling style, each evangelist added his own "curl"; each made the story relevant to his generation. This means, much to the scandal of some folks, they even put words in Jesus' mouth and made him say what he never would have said, could not have said, in his own lifetime.

To get a handle on this, we have to go back once more to the beginning. We live in a literary-print-visual world where the almighty word is fixed forever. And sealed. And certified. And copywritten. And archived. The ancients and the New Testament writers lived in a oral-aural storytelling world where the fluid word flowed. And expanded. And deepened. And conformed to the listeners. In the gospel, the core tradition, as we have carefully emphasized before, controls the details. Again, Santa could be made to say a lot of things he didn't actually say—things that relate to today's children, not yesterday's—but he could not be made to say anything contradictory to his identity. Jesus' eternal wisdom could be translated for a second generation's needs and it would still accurately reflect his teaching and mission, who he was. He could not be made to say anything contradictory to his identity.

We have trouble with this, but we do it ourselves more than we realize. And so, to use a common example, Stevie's mother says to him, "Remember, Stevie, my grandpa always said, 'Early to bed, early to rise, makes you healthy, wealthy and wise.' So, listen to grandpa and get ready for bed. I'll come and tuck you in." Grandpa never literally said any such thing. But grandpa staunchly believed that children need their rest. He was a foe of those parents who let their kids stay up to all hours watching television, and he saw to it that his kids went to bed early. That's the core tradition, as we might put it. Grandpa, whom little Stevie idolized, is a person of authority to Stevie, someone to listen to, who carries weight. Stevie's mother, acting like one of the evangelists, puts words in grandpa's mouth to address a reluctant bed-goer. The words are not factual but, in genuine storytelling fashion, they are true. They accurately reflect the grandpa tradition. In short, they are a distillation of the grandpa wisdom.

In a distinction a scholar would make, such accounts of grandpa—or Jesus—are not literal accounts, but they are historical. That is, they are rooted in the historical grandpa and Jesus. This also means that while some scholars claim they can detect the exactly quoted words of Jesus, that would be rare since, true to the oral tradition, Jesus' words would have necessarily undergone some variations, required by different situations, needs, and developing insights.

Now, suppose for the sake of argument, that in fact, grandpa was a libertine. He caroused, got drunk, stayed out all night, barreled in at all hours of the morning, slept it off all day, and didn't give a hoot about his kids. No way could you put the "early to bed, early to rise" words in his mouth. As we would say, the core tradition, attested by many witnesses (not the least of whom is grandma), would not allow such a perversion. He simply couldn't be made to say something that was contrary to the tradition. The only words you could honestly put into his mouth would be words like, "As Grandpa said, 'Live it up. You only go around once!'" But if grandpa was really the man in our initial example, then it's perfectly all right for mom to put words into his mouth for Stevie. She is accurately passing on grandpa's truth: the truth of his teaching and the truth of his life.

I spend time on this point because, again, people understandably are shocked to learn that the evangelists put words into Jesus' mouth. But as you can now see, it is quite legitimate to do so. There were still enough witnesses around to see that the tradition was reflected accurately and truthfully.

According to…

Keeping the oral tradition in mind helps us to come to terms with the variations and contradictions in the gospels. Here are some examples. In Mark 11:12–14, Jesus curses a fig tree, and when the apostles pass by the next day, they see it is all withered up. In Matthew 21:19, Jesus curses the fig tree and, lo and behold, it shrivels up right before the apostles' very eyes!

The skeptic cries, "See, two versions, each canceling the other out. How can you believe such stuff?" He says that because he went to Harvard and his world is a static, literary one. But story-tellers know their peers and they all know that Matthew is the Steven Spielberg of the evangelists because he loves to make Jesus' miracles much more dramatic; he simply could not wait till the next day for the tree to shrivel up. Just like Luke, who loves to inflate numbers for dramatic effect; in the Acts of the Apostles, thousands of people convert at the preaching of Peter and Paul, while there were probably only a couple dozen conversions. Was Bethlehem Jesus's hometown, as Matthew would lead us to believe? Or was it Nazareth, as Luke relates? Did Jesus go up to Jerusalem only once, according to Matthew, Mark, and Luke? Or several times, according to John? And what about all those con-flicting resurrection details: one angel or two angels at the tomb? Were they standing or sitting? Was the tomb already open or opened by an angel? What about the various messages of the angel? All these details are part of the oral development of the core tradition; all stretch to express the inexpressible.

Look at the birth stories. Nobody was there to record the birth of Jesus so how can we really know what happened? We certain-ly did not get the details from Mary or Joseph. It seems obvious that Joseph died before Jesus gathered his apostles, and there is no indication either in the gospels themselves or in the earliest centuries that Mary ever recounted the birth story. Besides, if she did tell the story of Jesus' birth, how in the world do you account for the two extremely different versions in Matthew and Luke? Mary couldn't have told such wildly diverse tales to two different people—at least not with a straight face. Nor could Joseph have told one version and Mary the other; you would then have the worst case of failed marital communication since Lucy and Desi.

The details of the birth stories are fanciful, as we have noted before. There's no public record, for example, of any astronomi-cal phenomenon such as the star that led the magi to Jesus (in spite of the annual Christmastime media articles), and no record of Augustus' census. Jesus is supposedly related to John the

Baptist, yet there is no indication that, as adults, they ever knew each other. In fact, John protests, "I myself did not know him" (Jn 1:33). The two genealogies are not even close. And so we can reasonably assume that, in writing about the birth of Jesus, Matthew and Luke have different purposes in mind.

To put it simply, Matthew's account is a storyteller's version of the Old Testament stories because he wants to present Jesus as a legal, authentic heir to the ancient promises. Notice Matthew's frequent use of Old Testament quotations from such revered authors as Isaiah, Jeremiah, and Hosea, and name-dropping such venerated notables as Abraham, Isaac, Jacob, David, and Solomon. And it is clear that St. Joseph and his dreams reflect Joseph the dreamer of the Old Testament. King Herod comes across as a disguised Pharaoh who tries to destroy the new Moses. And so, Matthew, in his overture to the gospel is previewing the story of Israel that Jesus will relive and complete.

In his overture, storyteller Luke likewise draws on the Old Testament. You only have to have a passing familiarity with those writings to see that the childless Elizabeth and Zechariah in Luke are but a disguised Sarah and Abraham. In fact, Zechariah mouths words similar to Abraham's in Genesis 15:8—"O Lord God, how am I to know that I shall possess it [the Promised land]?"—when he says, "How will I know this is so?" (Lk 1:18). Jesus' presentation in the Temple is a take-off on the prophet Samuel's presentation in the Temple, and Mary's great Magnificat is a copy, with some slight alterations, of Hannah's canticle in 1 Samuel 2:1–10.

These evangelists, Matthew and Luke, are trying to tell us that those old stories are now being played out fully in Jesus. It's what we identified before as *midrash*, that inventive combination of scriptural interpretation and reflection on contemporary events.

PART III

HISTORY, SACRED AND PROFANE

16.

Plot Lines

In the movie *Forrest Gump*, there is a scene where the wise simpleton, Forest, is talking to and shaking hands with President Lyndon Johnson. Of course, we know that it's not really Forrest Gump here, but an actor, Tom Hanks, playing Forrest Gump. And we know that Lyndon Johnson was long dead when this movie was made. Yet, by the wizardry of modern technology, the director, in the interest of the movie's plot, could bring them together.

To fit the needs of the plot and to make a coherent narrative, writers, both secular and sacred, sometimes move people, events, and chronology around a bit. Even modern historians do this to a certain extent. Being human, they are not as objective as we might think. For the most part, they conscientiously collect data and stories and look for patterns that connect the information. But at times they have to fill in with educated guesses when the data is meager or nonexistent. Then they have to go on assumptions and presumptions and may even have to create presumed dialogues. And, of course, many things will guide their final decision. For example, what is the purpose of the history they're writing? What is their point of view? What are their biases and presuppositions, whether open or hidden? What knowledge and experience do they bring to the task? The fact is, no matter how hard modern historians might try, they are products of their times and of the ongoing conditioning that has formed them from birth. They see reality as they have been taught to see it. As the Talmud says, "You don't see things as they are. You see things as *you* are."

All this applies to the biblical writers, a few of whom took on the role of historians—though hardly in the same sense as we understand the term. One example is the author we call the Deuteronomist in the Old Testament (most likely an elite committee of males) who gave us the Pentateuch, Chronicles, and both books of Samuel and of Kings. Another is Luke in the New Testament, with his book of Acts. But there is a huge difference between modern and ancient writers who tackle history. The modern historian relies on records, documents, old newspaper articles, letters, stories, archaeological digs, and the interpretation of all these elements. He or she must make choices (remember that: *they make choices*) and select the data (you can't include everything), analyze it, make comments and assessments on people and events (this or that president was a failure or success), and put it all into a reasonable (and filtered) narrative. Then they wait for their colleagues to critique their work.

Being pioneers, the ancient Mediterranean historians had very little data to draw on, very few records and very few critics. But they did have some court records and annals of the kings, and lots and lots of stories, and it was their task to sort them out. And like Herodotus and Thucydides (who are considered the fathers of history and who followed the ancient biblical historians by a hundred years), the Mediterranean historians wrote not merely to present the facts as they knew them, but in order to edify, persuade, and make moral and political points. In other words, contrary to the strictures of modern standards, they were openly partisan and made no bones about it.

We see this process of arranging the data to suit a purpose in the New Testament, as well. Mark, the first gospel writer, opens his work with, "The beginning of the good news of Jesus Christ, the Son of God" and so leaves no doubt as to kind of tale he is going to tell. So you see that, perhaps to your surprise, the biblical writers felt perfectly free to rearrange material to fit their agenda. They did not hesitate, for instance, to put long speeches into people's mouths in order to reveal their (the author's) motives. Look at Luke's speeches spoken by everyone in Acts, or the long speeches John put into Jesus' mouth. All this is what we call historiography: writing manipulated history with an agenda in mind. The adjective "manipulated" is not meant negatively here, but is meant to indicate that the writers who produced the Bible were not impartial and indeed were often passionate advocates.

Holy Propaganda

And that brings us to the central point of this chapter, one that must be made because, sooner or later, the observant reader will notice that some things don't "jell" when you compare so-called history book narratives. For example, if you compare the Acts of the Apostles with other parallel accounts, especially those from Paul who was some forty to fifty years nearer to the events that Luke describes, some things just don't fit.

We'll come back to Luke and Paul, but for now, we offer this caution: when we look at the biblical writers and the stories they told, we need to study their style, purpose, and ideologies in order to interpret them. As mentioned previously, we have to make the distinction between what is literal and what is historical in their writings. To do this we have to check out the pattern, the focus, the shape of the story they're telling, how they evaluated the data, and how that data is made to conform to that pattern. We must remember that they had bits and pieces of history and tradition, as well as many oral stories to go by. They had to bring some kind of order to these elements and so they bent events and chronology to fit that order, something that would surely violate modern canons. In other words, biblical story-telling is very much like the story of the Procrustean bed. That famous bed of lore was of one size and if you were not that size, you were either stretched or had your limbs lopped off to fit.

"Well," you might say, "that sounds pretty much like propaganda to me." And you're right: the Bible is propaganda. As we noted in the last chapter, it was written for in-house consumption—the "house" being the early Christian community—with the purpose of establishing and encouraging identity, meaning, and political loyalty. It is fueled by the utter conviction of Yahweh's presence and Jesus' vindication in the resurrection. The Bible is a faith document. It is not neutral. On the contrary, the biblical writers determinedly resorted to every kind of rhetorical device and figure of speech to tell their stories, as well as to convey their convictions. And so we must back off from too literal a reading of what they wrote.

You will notice that, like other historians both ancient and modern, the biblical authors focused on the high and mighty, the leaders, the great figures: Abraham, Moses, Joshua, David, Judas Maccabees, Jesus, Peter, Paul, and others. It's the same as Catholics, who have all kinds of histories about the popes and the saints, as well as Americans, with their histories about the Founding Fathers. Moreover, the ancient historians were less concerned about chronology (although they were concerned, as evident in the records and genealogies and epochs found in the Old Testament) than about an overall theme. (As we have seen, sometimes events and people were moved around like chess board figures to serve the theme.) They were much more interested in character than in information. In a word, much to our contemporary dismay, impartiality or objectivity were irrelevant to the biblical authors. Instruction, encouragement, loyalty, propaganda, and repentance were very much on their minds. There isn't any no-spin zone in the Bible; it's all spin, that is, writing slanted to appease a particular agenda. Let's look at one example from the New Testament (the same principles apply to the Old).

Luke, the Scheming Mind

Luke, the author of the third gospel, is also the author of the Acts of the Apostles, a kind of first history of the early Church—although again, the word "history" must be used loosely. He wrote Acts probably around 80-85 AD, fifty or more years after the events concerning Jesus and the beginning of the Christian community.

First, here are some facts about this man. We don't know exactly who Luke was. We *do* know that he is a second or third generation Christian, and therefore, he did not know Jesus. He did not know Peter. He did not know Paul and gives no indication that Paul ever wrote any letters. How could he not know that? This lack of knowledge is critical and surprising seeing how Luke wrote so extensively of Peter in the first fifteen chapters of his book, and about Paul in the remaining chapters. You would think he went to school with both of them or at least was good buddies with both. But these apostles had been long dead when Luke wrote and so he had to rely on written and oral sources.

Next, and this is important, Luke was very orderly, as he himself says: "I too decided, after investigating everything carefully from the very first, to write an orderly account for you…" (Lk 1:3). This love of order included a habit of always going through the proper channels.

Finally, Luke had a scheme in mind before he ever sat down to write (hence the subtitle of this section, "the scheming mind"), a storyline, a central theme, a framework within which to record his "history." That framework is what we might call a "stone dropped into the lake" pattern. That is to say, just as tiny waves ripple out to the farthest shore when a stone is dropped in the middle of a lake, so too Luke's gospel is dropped into a central place and ripples out to "the end of the earth" (Rome). For Luke, the stone is Christ and the lake is Jerusalem, the central place, the city of destiny. Everything in Luke is made to happen in Jerusalem and then ripple outward to Samaria, Corinth, Syria, Cilicia, Antioch, and finally to Rome, the center of the empire.

Jerusalem and its leadership are the glue, the driving motif, the theology, we might say, behind Luke's narrative. The movements in his gospel and in Acts converge on Jerusalem like the swell of a wave and then recede from it to terminate in Rome, the end of the earth as Luke knew it. After all God himself, who works in history, chose Jerusalem. It is a sacred place and so must be honored as the place from which God's revelation goes forth. And Luke sees to that.

In Luke's accounts it is from Jerusalem that the announcement of John's birth is made. Anna and Simeon prophesy in the Jerusalem temple. Jesus first appears in public to the temple teachers in Jerusalem. Near the end of his mission, it is toward Jerusalem that Jesus steadfastly marches; several times Luke describes Jesus with his face determinedly set toward that city. In contrast, Mark's gospel has Jesus, while on his way to Jerusalem, making a side visit to Tyre and Sidon. Luke omits that trip in his gospel because he wants nothing to interfere with that steady, uninterrupted march to Jerusalem. Once in Jerusalem, Jesus dies and rises again, then appears to his disciples there. Note that in Matthew and in John, the risen Lord appears to the disciples in Galilee, but Luke had to be consistent with his theme and so moves the appearance to Jerusalem. Finally, the Holy Spirit comes to the disciples in Jerusalem from which point the message ripples out to all the world.

For Luke, then, Jerusalem is the unifying force of the early Church. Thus, the people who are leaders of the church in Jerusalem are considered the "proper channels" through whom one must always go. All this supports Luke's predetermined fixed point, and when he collects the events and stories of Peter and Paul and the early church heroes and villains, they must all emphasize and validate that point. Therefore Luke does not hesitate to put speeches in people's mouths and freely rearrange chronology and geography to make it all work together. He is an author who is fitting a lot of collected stories into his framework, like jigsaw pieces into a puzzle.

Differing Versions

To illustrate how the predetermined framework plays out in Luke, let's look at two versions of a famous incident, the first from Acts 15:1–35, and the second written thirty years earlier by Paul. As Jesus' message began to spread and non-Jews were entering the "Way" (Luke's term), a question arose about whether or not the Gentile converts had to first become Jews before becoming Christian. Did they have to observe the kosher food laws? Did the males have to be circumcised? As more and more Gentiles entered the early Church, the issues became more urgent. How did the early Church react?

Let's look at the earliest version of these events, found in Paul's Letter to the Galatians (2:1–15). Paul was a vehement advocate of jettisoning all Jewish restraints. He recounts in Galatians that he himself went from Antioch to meet with the Jewish leaders at Jerusalem to get approval for his ministry—which was to be the first to preach to the uncircumcised Gentiles. (Remember, he was still under suspicion, having so recently oppressed the Christians.) In fact, Paul insists, nobody really gave him this commission; it came from God himself (Gal 1:11–12) and without consultation from anyone else (1:15–17). Paul states that he met privately with James and Peter who gave him the OK. Sometime after this encounter, Peter visits Antioch where he freely shares a meal with the non-circumcised Gentiles. But when people from the "other side" arrived (those who insisted on circumcision), Peter withdrew and Paul scolded Peter to his face for his hypocrisy. There are the facts as Paul describes them in his letter.

Luke comes along, not with a letter, but with a narrative, a story to tell. And notice not only the expansion but the need to work the episode into his Jerusalem framework. The account in Acts says that in fact Paul did not visit Jerusalem on his own initiative but rather, was officially "summoned" there. (There might be some truth here, because for all of his boasting that he was independent of and equal to the apostles at Jerusalem, Paul did find it necessary to touch base there.) Further, Acts clearly refers to some kind of public assembly where James makes the final decision. Peter makes a speech at that assembly indicating that God chose him to go to the Gentiles and that the Gentiles should be free of the "yoke that neither our ancestors nor we have been able to bear." Peter here is the initiating hero of the Gentiles. Finally, the assembly sends a letter to all the churches stating their decision not to enforce circumcision, and ordering the people not to eat meat that had been sacrificed to pagan idols.

Note several things here. In Luke unity is very important. Thus, the matter is brought to Jerusalem. The gathered assembly makes the decision. Speeches are made by the authority figures Peter and James. The proper channels are gone through as James, the leader of the Jerusalem church, makes the final comment and a letter is sent out, like an encyclical, from Jerusalem to all the other churches.

But in Paul, it's a different matter. He speaks of his own commission from God without any consultation with the other apostles or authority figures. He and he alone is the initiator. He decides to go up to Jerusalem; he is not summoned. He lays before them his mission, he does not receive it from them. He goes not as a subordinate but as an equal and claims that the leaders acknowledge his status, not the other way around. Furthermore, he insists that this was a private meeting, not the public assembly Luke portrays. Finally, Peter, according to Paul, is far from the initiator of the Gentile mission but on the contrary, is one who hypocritically allied himself with the "circumcision faction."

Harmonizing the Stories

How do you account for these differing versions? The short answer is that one is a very personal letter written by a sometimes intemperate Paul, while the other is a story narrative written much later by a cool Luke. Paul's is a first person account, very likely with some exaggeration and overly strong language. He is certainly closer to the events, and he was writing to people who obviously knew something of what was going on in the early church. Luke is writing some fifty years after Jesus' death and the events that took place in the early church. Consequently, Paul's account would appear to be more reliable even though we have to make some measured allowances for his polemics.

But in the storytelling context, we would say that the core tradition is clear in both these accounts, in spite of the discrepancies. There was in the early church a major dispute over circumcision and Gentile observance. There is no doubt about that. There is no doubt either that the fiery Paul was the initiator of a motion that Gentiles could remain uncircumcised, and that he indeed was a free-wheeling independent apostle outside the church structure. Then why did Luke change the details? For one thing, he simply may not have known about Paul's role. Or, if he did, he made changes to fit into his theological framework. Notice again, he gives no lines to Paul in Acts 15, and he makes Peter and James the main characters who bring Paul into the main church structure. Peter, one of the original Twelve to whom the keys had been given is made, as befits his status, to initiate the Gentile mission free of circumcision. The whole church is agreed and harmonious in sending out the letter which only asks that certain food rules be observed.

Luke's narrative agenda is operative here. He is writing about the formation and spread of the early church. Church unity, Jerusalem, the proper channels, and order are important to him. Fifty years after the fact he had to give an account of how the church spread from Jerusalem to other places, what happened when the Twelve were no longer around, and where along the way was it decided that Gentiles didn't have to be circumcised? That was the world Luke found when he started to write. He did not know the answers to these questions, yet he had to come up with answers in writing his history. So he collected what data he could and wove a narrative out of it.

Of course, he certainly knew that there were believers all over the Roman world. He knew how the Roman political system worked. He knew the names of church leaders and stories about the various apostles. He surely knew there was a debate somewhere along the line about circumcision and unclean foods. He had these facts even if he did not have the details, and he had to construct an orderly account out of all this, one that was within his own theological system. But the question remains: is what he came up with history? Many scholars are reluctant to call it so. We ourselves have difficulty in dealing with the obvious discrepancies. What's going on? Let's look.

The Structure

There are nearly thirty chapters in Acts. The first half of the book is devoted to Peter, and then he (like all the other apostles) is suddenly dropped and the second half is devoted to Paul. Jerusalem is the central focus in the first half, while places away from Jerusalem are the focus in the second half. You begin to sense an artificial framework operating, along with a sense of that "orderly account" Luke announced in the opening of his gospel. As we have seen, his organizing principle is Jerusalem, the sacred spot into which the stone was dropped. The story of Jesus and the pentecostal Spirit work within this sacred geography, and from it the Spirit flows to the end of the earth. (Notice the singular in Luke: the *end* of the earth not ends; that is, Rome.) All things had to ebb and flow from there, including major controversies and their resolutions.

For Luke, direction on important matters, like being released from Torah observance, could only come from proper official channels; that meant the mother church in Jerusalem. A major step such as a mission to the Gentiles could never have originated with a sole independent apostle like Paul. The community and Peter's role in it, were essential and critical, and any role Paul may have played must be subservient. (Remember, Luke did not have Paul's letters, including the one to the Galatians).

In reality, there was likely no such central debate about

Gentiles, circumcision, and kosher foods at Jerusalem; but on the other hand, there certainly were debates in Christian pockets throughout the empire about these topics. Luke has simply coalesced them into one central debate at Jerusalem to stay true to his framework of a united, harmonious Christian community centered there. The details are manipulated to fit Luke's agenda, and the presence of the Holy Spirit is inexorably behind this steady ripple to "the end of earth." Everything is bent to this meaning, this interpretation. Remember, in Luke's gospel introduction he told his patron, Theophilus, that he wrote "so that you may have the assurance concerning the things about which you have been instructed" (1:4). As the commentator in the *New Interpreter's Study Bible* aptly put it,

> For the Gospel writer, narrative is not "facts" but proclamation. Luke's concern, then, is to provide a faithful accounting of the significance of what has taken place, not to prove that these things actually happened.

The core tradition remains intact: the spread of the Church beyond Jerusalem, the infusion of Gentile converts, the debates over entering through the Jewish door, the rejection of circumcision, apostolic authority. Luke's proclamation "history" of these events is not what we would tolerate in our modern view. But, to the ancients, it was normative. Life was not objective or neutral. The ancients regarded historical reality with a permeating sense of faith and their accounts are not always to be taken literally. There is a core narrative there, and they were anxious not over what it said but what it meant as seen through the prism of a persistent God.

I agree that sometimes you might be tempted to think that so much of the Bible seems to be a variation of that old (pre-politically correct) vaudeville joke:

"There I was, surrounded by ten thousand hostile Indians!"
"How many?"
"Well, maybe five thousand."
"How many"

"Well, there I was, surrounded by five hundred hostile Indians!"

"How many?"

"Well, maybe seventy-five."

"How many?"

"Well, maybe thirty."

"How many?'

"Well, I said to the Old Squaw...."

Luke is famous for inflating numbers that inflate the power of the Holy Spirit to lead the church to such wondrous expansion. And indeed, there was expansion, and there were leaders who brought the good news beyond Jerusalem to eventually captivate the Western world. History or historiography, something happened—and Someone was behind it all.

17.

His-Story

L et's continue the theme of the previous chapter and explore more fully the question, "Told or written, are the stories true in this story collection we call the Bible?" The question is timely because, as we cited in chapter 2, we are increasingly faced with the issue of authenticity. In popular national magazines (especially at Christmas and Eastertime) and on the Discovery Channel or Frontline or numerous other television programs, it is commonplace to encounter people voicing doubts about the Bible in general and Jesus in particular. These media people raise troublesome issues for the ordinary faithful who seldom have the critical tools to refute these contentions or put them in context. Most of the issues center on history and the comments go something like this: archaeology cannot prove there was an Exodus or that Abraham, Isaac, or Jacob ever existed. The evidence is that they are fictitious characters or, if they did exist, they were unrelated petty chieftains from different eras, heroes of some local tribes who became inflated into mighty patriarchs and made to be related as father, son, and grandson.

Moses, if he existed, surely did not write the Pentateuch any more than the apostle Matthew wrote the gospel of Matthew. David probably did exist, although according to the records (or lack of them), as a local Mafia-type henchman—hardly as the mighty king of a vast territory. David's son, Solomon, according to the Bible, was a boy wonder. He was both master builder and insatiable accumulator. He drank out of golden goblets, outfitted his soldiers with golden shields, maintained a fleet of sailing ships to seek out exotic treasures, kept a harem of 1,000 wives and concubines, and spent thirteen years building a palace and a richly decorated temple to house the Ark of the Covenant.

Yet not one goblet, not one brick, has ever been found to indicate that such a reign existed. So the piercing questions fly: if Solomon of fabulous wealth, renowned wisdom and extensive empire reigned for almost forty years, why are there no inscriptions from his reign, no mention of him in other extra-biblical records? If he engaged in international trade and imported luxury goods, why are so few of these goods found in his supposed fortresses of Hazor, Gezer, and Megiddo? Why are there only meager remains from his supposed capital of Jerusalem, the centerpiece of his building expansion? Conclusion: do we have here historical memory, or legends and folktales circulated long after ancient Israel had come and gone?

There's more. As noted before, Joshua did not topple the walls of Jericho with his trumpets, for the records show that these walls were down some two hundred years before Joshua supposedly arrived on the scene. Jesus' ministry is listed variously as one year to three years. We know almost nothing about him outside of the gospels. The lists of the twelve apostles are never the same. We have two accounts of Judas' death. The New Testament writers show Jesus quoting the Hebrew Scriptures with precision but they change (mangle?) them to suit their purposes. And it goes on and on. Can this book we call the Bible, with so many contradictions, errors, and unverifiable statements, be history?

History or His-story?

It all depends on what you mean by history. For the sake of discussion, we can say that, over the centuries, there have been three phases to the understanding of history in relation to the Bible.

Phase I is the literal phase, the one that has endured for almost two millennia and in some quarters today, still vigorously does. This phase defines history as "the true story of the past" in the same sense that a court of law seeks to establish the facts in a case. In Phase I, the Bible as history accurately and objectively portrays the facts. Everything in it is literally true. Abraham, Isaac, and Jacob were related. Moses wrote the Pentateuch, even though it took a thousand years to attach his name to it. David was a mighty, international king even though there is only one minor (ambiguous) mention of the house of David outside the Bible. Solomon was one of the greatest kings ever. The occupation of Canaan happened just as described in the book of Joshua, even though research shows it was not a stupendous, instantaneous invasion but rather a slow assimilation. Phase I is the fundamentalist's prism and is not to be dismissed out of hand.

But along came Phase II, which entered with the Enlightenment and endures today among the intellectuals (and among us, for the most part). The claim here is that in no way is the Bible history. Research and archaeology have conclusively shown that the Bible is a work of nationalistic propaganda whose so-called historical facts are bogus; what facts may indeed be there are twisted to fit the agenda of the writers. In no way do the facts of real history fit in with the fictional history of the Bible. One has to be radically skeptical when one reads the Bible looking for history.

The Phase II folk have a point—if you define history as "a true story of the past." But suppose you take the words of the renowned historian, Jan Huizinga, who defines history as "the intellectual form in which a civilization renders account to itself of its past." Now the definition is cast wider. An account of the past does indeed have to have some relationship with literal events, but is that all? Is there nothing else that defines a civilization's past and accounts for its present? What about its traditions, its rituals, its fictions, its superstitions, its legends, its stories, even its lies? Surely all these reveal something about a people and their need to define themselves in they way they do. What made them use their imaginations that way? What does their propaganda say about them?

For example, any accurate history of the Third Reich must not only include the "facts," the dates and times of the rise and fall of Hitler's ghastly empire, but surely must include the propaganda, the "media spin." The lies, the persuasions, the appeals, the false promises—all reveal deeper meanings and intent and cannot be bypassed because they do not portray "facts." What about the jokes and the coded stories surreptitiously passed around the occupied people? Don't they tell us something? Don't they, too, tell a story?

The word "history" originally meant just what its etymology suggests: his-story. But the Phase II people connected what they should have left separated. They deleted the hyphen and made the conjoined word "history" to refer only to the facts, leaving "story" to refer to the narrative, with the implication that it had little value. History in this sense meant that only the facts counted, and the works of historians like Thucydides and the Hebrew authors of the Exodus were valuable only for the factual material they contained, not the stories they told. And that was a loss.

Phase III is what is unfolding now. We might call this the postmodern phase. It is more open to seeing history in its original hyphenated sense, that is, it contains both facts and stories. There is "objectivity" (if that is possible) and there is imagination. Both say something. Both are revelatory. It's not either-or but both-and. Phase III asks that, even where there is factual error, subjective interpretation, and artificial history, don't these very things give evidence of the self-identity of a people? Let me offer a modern example of his-story.

An Heroic Tale

Most people know something of the great epic of Masada. The storyline, to refresh your memory, goes like this: noble Jewish rebels retreated to Masada, a high plateau in the desert near the Dead Sea, after the Romans burned Jerusalem in the year 70 AD, and for two years they harried the Romans encamped nearby. The Romans finally built an earthen ramp to reach Masada, forcing the Jews into the dilemma of either handing over their families to slavery or to the sword, or of committing collective suicide. Rather than surrender, they heroically chose the latter.

Such a courageous stance was given widespread credence when Yigael Yadin, Israel's most celebrated archaeologist, excavated Masada. He told the whole world that Masada was a sign of Israel's resolve to face its enemies, and an apt symbol for the fledgling state of Israel. Masada quickly fell into nationalistic lore to the extent that Israeli soldiers sometimes swore their oath of allegiance on the mountain, shouting "Masada shall not fall again!"

But in a Phase II sense, that's not quite the truth. In a new book, *Sacrificing Truth: Archaeology and the Myth of Masada*, a professor at Hebrew University accuses Yadin of deliberately distorting his findings to "provide Israelis with a spurious historical account of heroism." Interestingly, Yadin's defenders admit that he embellished the facts but, they say, he can be forgiven considering his popularity and his own fervent nationalism. Like other Jewish archaeologists Yadin was anxious to provide Israeli pioneers of the mid-1900s with heroic tales to document Zionist claims to the land. But his nationalism got in the way of the facts. The so-called defenders and patriots of Masada, far from being heroes, turn out to be a group of vicious assassins who killed both Romans and Jews. Josephus himself described them as belonging to a Jewish sect knows as *Sicarii* (meaning "dagger"), who had murdered over 700 women and children. They were hardly noble heroes; they were terrorists.

The Masada myth, however, is so entrenched in the popular imagination, so enshrined in Israel's national consciousness, so embedded in the cultural icons of movies, songs, and TV specials, that to suggest it's all wrong might bring the worst of all cultural anathemas: charges of anti-Semitism. Nevertheless, the tale of Masada is just that: a tale, a national symbol. Phase I embraces it. Phase II dismisses it. Phase III considers it.

Phase III says that, even though these are not the actual "facts," the story itself reveals something of the times, the needs of a people, the motivation of the archaeologist, and the struggles of a nation. The story, while not literal, is indeed historical. There was a Masada, there was a group of Jews camped on its top, there were Roman soldiers bent on capturing this plateau and there was a bloody confrontation. The interpretation of these facts might not be "history" and the professor is right to expose that fact, but it surely is "his-story" in the same way that the non-historical Paul Bunyan and Johnny Appleseed are part of our-story and help define our national character.

This doesn't mean that we have to be indifferent to factual truth and say it doesn't count. It means that, from the storytelling point of view that is so much a part of the Bible, we must look behind the facts, whether they are actual, distorted, or rearranged, and come back to our old saying: ask not, What does it say? but, What does it mean? Why does the story, factual or embellished, exist to begin with? What is it trying to tell the group for whom it is meant?

The Phase III mentality doesn't accept all of Phase I and criticizes Phase II, then tries to combine the both. Phase III says we need to take the text as it is and focus within the text itself. If we cannot know history, we can know his-story. If we cannot swallow the so-called "facts" we can accept the narrative, the storyline, and try to parse its meaning as God's word. In other words, Phase III goes on the assumption that the Bible is in fact a story, the story of a particular community, and we have to enter into this story through the life of the community it portrays and the lives of its characters.

After all, even we moderns accept the mixture of fiction and fact in Shakespeare, the theatre, and the "based on a true story" byline of the movies and television. Two authors might help us get a grasp on this. One is Margaret Ralph who in her book, *And God Said What?* explains the incident of Moses and his rod which drove back the Red Sea.

A modern reader might well ask, "Well, which was it? Was this a natural event, a wind, or a supernatural event, Moses and his rod?" The question ignores the intent of the authors. The distinction between natural and supernatural is irrelevant. In both accounts we are dealing with an event in which God's presence was experienced. The difference between the methods through which God acted—through the wind or through the more dramatic and marvelous action in which Moses raised his rod—illustrates the exaggeration that is characteristic of legend. In the later version the author has embellished the story using exaggeration to make Moses' role more dramatic.

Remember that the legends were told and retold not merely to recall the past but to affect a present audience. To embellish a legend with marvelous details is to make it all the more interesting and inspiring to the next generation. In most legends exaggeration is used to build up a human hero. In these legends, however, the religious purpose of the author is always present. It is not really Moses, but God acting through Moses, who is being glorified. The author wishes to inspire his audience with the marvelous nature of God's intervention in the history of God's people. Their God is a God who saves.

Pulitzer prize winner Jack Miles expresses the same thought in his book simply entitled *God: A Biography:*

No responsible historian believes that at the time of the Exodus the Israelites actually outnumbered the Egyptians or that a company of 4 or 5 million people made its way through the desert and into Canaan. Despite the lack of any historical record outside the Bible, most historians do not believe that the story of the Exodus is a total fabrication. But were it an event of the size that the Bible reports, the likelihood of its leaving no record outside the Bible would be small. For the literary effect of the Book of Exodus to be what its authors intended, however, it is essential that readers imagine the numbers that the text reports rather than the ones that historians may, on other evidence, have good reason to believe. Historians of England have good reason to believe that Richard III was not the monster that Shakespeare made him out to be in the play that bears his name. Nonetheless, if the play is to work as Shakespeare intended, the villain must be allowed to be a villain.

The same, analogously, goes for the Book of Exodus. Cecil B. De Mille's *The Ten Commandments*, with its mighty throng crossing the sea, may be more true to the intended literary effect of the Book of Exodus than scholarship's reconstruction of a band of minor tribes slipping through the marsh.

It will be most helpful if, once more, you remember that the Bible was not written for the public. It was not written for outsiders. It was an in-house production intended for adherents to the belief in God and in God breaking into their history. For those who do not share this viewpoint, biblical history is bunk.

For these believers, however, history was always his-story and so exaggerations, inflation, legends—anything, in short, that underscored God's activity and presence—was grist for the storytelling mill. As Jack Miles put it, if the biblical stories are to work as reminders of God's claim on the chosen people and of their claim on God, then every Cecil B. DeMille strategy must be allowed, every device permitted that renders an account of its past, affirms its present, and lends hope to its future. History? Not always. His story? Always.

18.

WHY STORIES?

This final chapter spells out more fully the issues of history raised in the last two chapters. It once more asks, why? Why did the Hebrews gather and tell stories to begin with? The short answer is that they did it for the same reasons all peoples do. Here are some of these reasons.

First, stories reflect the beliefs of a people. Israel, like other peoples, wanted to claim its God as the Lord of history. It wanted to closely correlate the story of its God and the activity of its God with human history because it wanted to show that Yahweh is the Lord of history and is in charge of where history is going. (The Hebrews had a linear view of history, which they got from the Sumerians, in contrast to, say, the cyclical view of the Egyptians.) The Hebrews wholeheartedly believed that their God, who was on their side, directed the course of human history—a sentiment, in fact, shared by other nations such as Syria, with its god, Assaur, or the Babylonians with their god, Marduk.

Second, stories preserve identity. Israel told its stories as a conscious political act in order to preserve its unique identity. The

Hebrew people accomplished this by carefully defining themselves over and against the culture of their day. The fact is, their
faith in and allegiance to the true and living God produced an
abrasiveness with surrounding cultures who had more earthly
allegiances (the old cry, "They're different!"). So they had to
come up with stories that not only justified what set them apart
but also encouraged the people to *stay* apart. The early Christians,
by the way, did the same thing. They told their stories in order to
set themselves over and against the imperial emperor-worshiping
court of Rome. Through their stories they drew the line between
themselves and the empire.

Third, stories nurture the beliefs and practices of a culture.
Israel told its story to protect its adherents from influences of the
surrounding culture. In discussing the political community-
forming nature of the biblical story, well-known Old Testament
theologian Walter Brueggemann, puts it this way:

> Israel's narrative is a partisan polemical narrative. It is con-
> cerned to build a counter community—counter to the
> oppression of Egypt, counter to the seduction of Canaan,
> counter to every imperial pretense. There is nothing in their
> narrative that will appeal to outsiders who belong to anoth-
> er consensus, or who share different ethos, and participate
> in another [truth-system]. To such persons, Israel's narratives
> are silly, narrow, scandalous and obscurantist....[The] Torah
> intends to nurture insiders who are willing to risk a specific
> universe of discourse and cast their lot there. (quoted by
> William Willimon, in *The Creative Word*).

A sidebar: both Jews and Catholics were once decidedly marked
as different from the surrounding culture—so much so that, in the
case of Catholics, a rash of hostile literature flourished telling how
Catholics could not be loyal Americans. They were considered too
different, too "foreign," too noticeably odd with their missals, fish
on Friday, Mass on Sunday, Latin, confession, large families,
medals, saints, novenas, candles, incense, vestments, and mis-
sions. Today, both Jews and Catholics are virtually indistinguish-

able from the general culture. According to every poll, Catholics consume, vote, have sex, practice birth control, have abortions, get divorced, build large houses, drive SUVs, fight to get their children into the "right" schools, and climb ever upward exactly like everyone else. And three-fourths of them do not celebrate the Eucharist, the very core of the faith. For the first time in American history more Protestants go to church than Catholics (Gallup poll, November 2003). In short, there is no measurable distinction between Catholics and other people. In our terms, the story line (the identifying "mega-story") has broken down or more accurately, been replaced by another mega-story: consumerism. (Read, for example, *One Nation Under Goods*, by James J. Farrell, and *The Progress Paradox*, by Greg Easterbrook.)

Fourth, stories provide meaning, motivation, and hope, and the biblical stories (again, like other people's stories or national myths) gave these to the Hebrew people. According to Jack Zipes:

> Certainly, this is one of the reasons why the narrators kept these tales alive, for the words have a relevance not only within the plot and narrative strategy of the tale, but they bring out the pertinence of the stories in such a way that the hearers will remember to tell what has a meaning for their lives. The words of the tale touch them emotionally and are absorbed by them, for they are weapons of the weak. They bear messages for survival. They bare some naked truths and demand that we pay attention to why we use words the way we do, and how we can use words to resolve discomforting social conditions. Words are given in trust. Words form the curses, spells, and vows that determine the action of all the protagonists.

Tales tell what life is about, what we are about, how we are to live, where we are going.

Fifth, stories forge community. We are united with all those who believe as we do and uphold the same values enshrined in our stories. We are part of a larger picture, threads in the same fabric. Think of the American myths: the Revolutionary War, Washington, Lincoln, Teddy Roosevelt, Paul Bunyan, Johnny

Appleseed, Molly Pitcher, the Alamo, how the West was won, and so on. These myths of American independence and self-made citizens who shucked parliaments and popes, royalty and titles, customs and restraints, tell us who we are. Religious stories have this function, as well. (Or had. In modern times, identity is the function of corporate brand names. We are bonded globally on the brands we prefer, can afford, and consume.)

Six, stories provide guidelines for behavior or ethics. We do what we do because we're compelled by the demands of the myth. If you buy into the Hebrew myth, for example, you faithfully observe the Sabbath and eat only kosher food. In the Catholic myth of previous generations, you could not eat meat on Friday, women had to cover their heads in church, and all had to confess their sins once a year. Those public acts not only set you apart but provided concrete guidelines for moral conduct.

Finally, stories provide healing. As Joy Carol observes in her book, *Journeys of Courage*:

> We live in very turbulent and violent times. Many of our communities have been damaged or disconnected in some way. We yearn to feel more wholesome and peaceful, to find a reason for hope, to be more courageous. We may need and want to change our situation, but we are uncertain how to go about doing so. Through the examples found in stories, we can be helped to see various options for action. Stories have the ability to fill us with all kinds of possibilities. They can encourage us to move ahead by telling us truths about what has worked before, what has failed, what we can try ourselves, what we should avoid.
>
> For centuries, storytelling has been used as a powerful and beneficial tool in the healing process. Healing stories can touch our hearts and help us understand that life is a series of challenges—not all good, not all bad. Healing stories can help us expand our consciousness so that we can see our lives and the world in new ways. Yes, telling and hearing stories can be powerful medicine.

Carol quotes a woman from Northern Ireland who has dedicated her life to healing the terrible wounds of the last thirty years of hate, killing, and strife in her land. She says,

> We can encourage the rest of the world if they hear our good stories, our stories of courage, of hope, of forgiveness, of coming together, of new life. I feel that healing stories need to be shouted form the housetops.

Israel, beleaguered, needed the stories of Abraham's faithfulness, Moses' steadfastness, David's repentance, Ezra's restoration, Daniel's wisdom, and above all, Yahweh's slowness to anger and quickness to forgive. The troubled communities Jesus left behind—riddled with the disagreements Paul so ardently bemoaned, along with false teachers, ejection from the synagogue, persecution, defection, and martyrdom—were in dire need of healing stories.

How welcomed must have been the stories of Jesus healing Peter's mother-in-law, praising the widow's mite, relating tales of lost sheep and prodigal fathers, raising Lazarus, weeping over Jerusalem, forgiving the paralyzed man, carrying his own cross manfully, offering reconciliation to the Good Thief, and promising his own resurrection for those who are persecuted and maligned because they carry his name. How the distressed Christians must have sought out every story, clung to every detail! In Jesus, they too would learn of endless possibilities and find a reason for hope and courage. His message indeed was "good news" where there was so much bad news. The gospel sustained them.

The bottom line is that the Bible is a bunch of different stories, legends, myths, poetry, fiction, and so on, told and gathered over many centuries, that have one common motif: they define a people. It goes without saying, not all the stories have to be factual. They just have to be true for their adherents. They have to be told and told often (and written down) so that this particular people know not only who they are but also who they are in relationship to the deity they call Yahweh. That is why the essence of the yearly Jewish Passover and the Christian Holy Week is the story.

Conclusion

I would like to conclude this last chapter with a reference to the first chapter. It is something that more properly should be developed in a book on spirituality so I'll make but brief mention of it. We said in that first chapter that revelation is basically concerned with a Person, not a proposition. Revelation is God's self-disclosure. God is the focal point. I also mentioned in another chapter that our old Judeo-Christian biblical mega-story—the large, overarching fund of metaphors and meanings enshrined in our literature, laws, celebrations, and culture—has been replaced by a new mega-story: that of consumerism.

Consumption is what truly defines humanity today, and our identity is centered on brand names and the ability to consume as much as possible. The old Mort Sahl remark is more apt than ever: "Ask a Californian who he is and he points to his car." Well, that truism has become both national and global. The manner and means of consumption are the standard of a successful life and announce who we are. I don't have shoes, I have a Jimmy Choos. I don't have a dress, I have an Yves St. Laurent. I don't have a handbag, I have a Gucci. I don't have a suit, I have an Armani; I don't have a car, I have a super-powered XL 70; I don't have a painting, I have a Jackson Pollock. I don't have a closet, I have several bins in those huge self-storage units that have sprung up like weeds all over the American landscape to handle our excess. Well, you get the point. We are consumerist to the core and therein lies our identity.

Thus, along with our "scientific" mentality, we also bring this consumerist attitude to the Bible stories and to their message. So now, these stories are not really about God and God's demands—but about us! The stories have been co-opted to help us fulfill our potential, find our bliss, get ahead, pass the competition, feel better, and shape up. Look at how the average parish caters to self-fulfillment agendas and entertainment needs. There are very few parishes that leave you with the profound notion that religion is all about God, not ourselves; there are very few with a clear teaching on how we must become less and God must become more. There is no Pauline sense that, "It is no longer I that live, but that Christ lives in me," or identification with Jesus' prayer that "not my will, but yours be done" and "I always do the will of him who sent me." In short, the biblical stories have been tamed into self-help categories and justifications. A Presbyterian minister put his finger on it:

Two things that are basic to the Christian life are unfortunately counter to most things American. First, Christian spirituality, the contemplative life, is not about us. It is about God. The great weakness of American spirituality is that it is all about us: fulfilling our potential, getting the blessings of God, expanding our influence, finding our gifts, getting a handle on principles by which we can get an edge over the competition. The more there is of us, the less there is of God.

Christian spirituality is not a life-project for becoming a better person. It is not about developing a so-called deeper life. We are in on it, to be sure, but we are not the subject. Nor are we the action. The major American innovation in the congregation is to turn it into a consumer enterprise. Americans have developed a culture of acquisition, an economy that is dependent on wanting and requiring more. We have a huge advertising industry designed to stir up appetites we didn't even know we had. We are insatiable. If we have a nation of consumers, obviously the quickest and most effective way to get them into our churches is to identify what they want and offer it to them. Satisfy their fantasies, promise them the moon, recast the gospel into consumer terms—entertainment, satisfaction, excitement and adventure, problem-solving—whatever. We are the world's champion consumers, so why shouldn't we have state-of-the-art consumer churches?

There's only one thing wrong: This is not the way that God brings us into conformity with the life of Jesus Christ. This is not the way that we become less and Jesus becomes more. This is not the way in which our lives become available to others in justice and service. The cultivation of consumer spirituality is the antithesis of a sacrificial "denying yourself" congregation. A consumer church is an anti-Christ church. It's doing the right thing—gathering a congregation—but doing it in the wrong way. This is not the way to develop a contemplative life, a life in which the Jesus way and the Jesus truth are congruent. (Eugene H. Peterson, from an article in *The Christian Century*.)

Enough of what belongs in another book. I just wanted to remind you that reading (listening to) the biblical stories can be dangerous to your status as a self-referral consumer; that the stories, after all, are not really about us and our need to win the lottery but about God.

Finally, it is only fitting that I should end a book called *In the Beginning There Were Stories* with a story. It hearkens back to our first chapter; namely, that, when all is said and done, the stories of the Bible are revelation. They are revelation, remember, not of doctrines and propositions, but of a Person, of Erik from the Christmas story in chapter one, of Someone who declared, "Behold, I have loved you with an everlasting love" and who inspired the sacred authors to do whatever they could to get the point across, no matter how wild, how creative, or how extravagant. Wisely, the authors, who had a choice, chose not briefs or reports or "objective" printouts. They chose story.

Once long ago in a distant land, a prince was riding through a forest far from his home with his company of soldiers, looking for new lands to conquer. Quite suddenly he came upon clearing in the trees. There before him stretched a meadow leading to a glorious hill. The meadow and hill were covered blossoming trees, bushes, and wildflowers. At the top of the hill was a castle that seemed made of pure gold. It sparkled so in sunlight that the prince was nearly blinded. Fascinated, the prince signaled to his regiment, and together they rode closer and closer, and up the hill toward the castle. The birds sang sweetly, the perfume of flowers was lovely As they drew near the castle, he saw that a window opened for a moment in the wall and a face appeared, a face that shone more brilliantly than the sun and yet more gently than any flower. Then it was gone. Instantly he fell in love.

He knocked upon the castle door. "Who is there?" came a voice softer than the bluest sky. "It is I, Prince Rindlelleart. I am known throughout the land for my bravery. My armies are the strongest. My castle is but two days' ride from here. May I please come and be with you?"

"There is only room for one of us here," was the reply.

He left downcast and in his desperation he sought the wisdom of a wise woman. "Perhaps your armies intimidate her," she suggested.

"Of course," he thought. He returned to the castle alone and knocked upon the door.

"Who is there?" came the sweet voice.

"It is I, the prince, alone," he replied humbly.

"There is only room for one of us here," said the sweet voice.

He went away again, dejected and confused. He roamed the wilderness for some years until he met a famous wizard. "Perhaps she cannot know you with all of your armor and weaponry," he suggested.

"Of course," said the prince. So he returned and laid down his armor, his shield, and his sword. He walked humbly to the castle door and knocked. "Who is there?" asked the voice.

"It is I, your humble servant. No soldier, just a man."

"There is only room for one of us here," came the reply.

For seven more years the prince wandered alone in the wilderness, forsaking his kingdom, thinking only of his beloved. He sought wisdom only from the stars in the sky and the wildness inside him.

Finally one day the prince returned to the castle on the hill. He had no armies, no armor, no horse. He walked up the hill, past the bushes heavily laden with fruit, and knocked upon the door.

"Who is there?" came the sweet voice.

The prince took a breath, and said, "It is thou."

And the door was opened to him.

I suppose one could say that the story means that true spiritual growth occurs when one loves the Beloved more than oneself. Or, it could mean that, in approaching the Bible, one has to discard the "armor and weaponry" of the modern "scientific" mindset, the literalist tunnel vision, and approach only with a vulnerability to the magic of the imagination.

Or on the other hand, it could mean a thousand other things. Hey, after all, it's a story.

BIBLIOGRAPHY

Aurelio, John. *Colors!* New York: Crossroad Publishing Co, 1993.

Bausch, William J. *Storytelling, Faith and Imagination.* Mystic, CT: Twenty-Third Publications, 1984.

——— *More Telling Stories, Compelling Stories.* Mystic, CT: Twenty-Third Publications, 1993.

Brown, Raymond. *101 Questions and Answers on the Bible.* Mahwah, NJ: Paulist Press, 1990.

Buechner, Frederick. *The Hungering Dark.* New York: Seabury Press, 1969.

Carol, Joy. *Journeys of Courage.* Notre Dame, IN: Sorin Books, 2004.

Canfield, Jack, ed. *Chicken Soup for the Christian Soul.* Deerfield Beach, FL: Health Communicaions Inc., 1997.

Denby, David. *Great Books: My Adventures with Homer, Rousseau, Woolf, and Other Indestructible Writers of the Western World.* Riverside, NJ: Simon and Schuster, 1996.

Hill, Geoffrey. *New & Collected Poems: 1952-1992.* Boston, MA: Houghton Mifflin and Penguin Books, Ltd, 1994.

Holt, David and Bill Mooney, eds. *Ready to Tell Tales.* Little Rock, AR: August House, 1994. Ltd.

Krivak Andrew. "Author of 'The Rings': Tolkein's Catholic Journey." *Commonweal.* December 19, 2003.

Lumet, Sidney. *Making Movies*. New York: Vintage Books, 1995.

McDonagh, Melanie. *The Tablet* 23/30. December, 2000.

McDonald, E.D. *The Posthumous Papers of D. H. Lawrence*. New York: Viking Press, 1936.

Miles, Jack. *God: A Biography*. New York: Vintage Books, 1996.

Pearmain, Elisa Davy, ed. *Doorways to the Soul*. Cleveland, OH: The Pilgrim Press: 1998.

Ralph, Margaret. *And God Said What?* Mahwah, NJ: Paulist Press, 1986.

Rausch, Thomas. *Who is Jesus?* Liturgical Press, 2003.

Zipes, Jack. *Beautiful Angiola: the Great Treasury of Sicilian Folk and Fairy Tales*. Collected by Laura Gronzenbach. New York: Routledge, 2004.